CUMBRIA ARCHAEOLOGICAL RESEARCH 1

ST. MARY'S ABBEY, HOLME CULTRAM, ABBEYTOWN, CUMBRIA: ARCHAEOLOGICAL AND HISTORICAL INVESTIGATIONS

Jan Walker and Mark Graham

With contributions by
Pat Bull, Lawrence Butler, Peter Davey, Jo Dawson, Alison Goodall,
Thomas Mace, John Mattinson, Don O'Meara, Tim Padley, Kate Rennicks,
Rachel Tyson, Joanne Wilkinson and Richard Wilson

CUMBERLAND AND WESTMORLAND

ANTIQUARIAN AND ARCHAEOLOGICAL SOCIETY

2013
Series editor: Marion McClintock

Cumberland and Westmorland
Antiquarian and Archaeological Society

CUMBRIA ARCHAEOLOGICAL RESEARCH REPORTS NO. 4

Series editor
Marion McClintock

© West Cumbria Archaeological Society, 2013

ISBN 978-1-873124-61-1

Printed by
Badger Press, Bowness on Windermere
2013

CONTENTS

LIST OF ILLUSTRATIONS

Figures *page*

Plates

Tables

PREFACE

The Cumbria Archaeological Research Reports, of which this is the fourth, are intended to bring into the public domain archaeological reports on sites within Cumbria that fall between a length suitable for a journal article and the size and nature of material appropriate for a monograph. Some may cover work that has taken some years to write up, while others will put on record work that is current, as is the case for St Mary's Abbey, Holme Cultram. The Cumberland and Westmorland Antiquarian and Archaeological Society is delighted to publish the work of archaeological investigations at the Abbey between 2006 and 2010 and their subsequent analysis carried out by the West Cumbria Archaeology Society, with the financial support of the Heritage Lottery Fund, the Solway Sustainable Development Fund, and Natural England.

The Abbey dedicated to St Mary at Holme Cultram was a Cistercian house of 1150, founded by King David of Scotland. The mother church was at Melrose, and there is a suggestion of an earlier, timber structure, and of cultural links across the Irish Sea, while the original red sandstone of its construction almost certainly came from the Scottish side of the Solway Firth and down the River Waver. On 6th March 1538 the house was dissolved, despite its relative wealth, and it owes its survival to the existing accommodation of a parish congregation in the nave, which continues actively to this day.

Some archaeological work was carried out at the Abbey at intervals between 1870 and 1925, but modern techniques had not been applied to the structure or to the finds. The recent extended period allowed for investigations that revealed first-hand evidence of the monastic buildings to the south of the Abbey, using up-to-date archaeological technology, including important finds of architectural stone, coloured window glass and a wide range of pottery. The discussion sets these within their historical context and that of other religious houses across England and beyond. The publication is therefore of considerable interest in its own right and in providing a baseline for any further investigations in the future.

The CWAAS wishes to publish a report of this kind at least once a year, and welcomes suggestions for further topics.

Marion McClintock
January 2013

ACKNOWLEDGEMENTS

We are very grateful to the Heritage Lottery Fund, Solway Sustainable Development Fund, and Natural England, which financed this project. The parish of Holme Cultram, the church and in particular the Revd David Tembey, the team vicar, have been continuously supportive, allowing us to use the excellent facilities of the Abbey during excavation. The farmer, Kevin McDonagh, has also freely given his permission for work and helped with backfilling.

Thanks are due to all the members of the West Cumbria Archaeological Society, around 70 in number, who took part in the excavations, pot washing and marking, sorting of finds, workshops and archival research. Particular thanks are due to committee members for support and help in organisation, and our treasurer, Maureen Denby, for supervising our finances.

The report has been compiled, edited and partially written by Jan Walker, co-director of excavations, with Mark Graham of Grampus Heritage Ltd. Mark Graham has supported the Society and undertook the magnetometry survey and report and has co-written the excavation reports, discussion and conclusion. Pat Bull, WCAS secretary and Kate Rennicks, compiled the historical background, with archival research by Maureen McNamara, Ray and Sally Newton, Maggie Sergeant and Jan Walker. Other members deserving particular mention are Mark Lawson, Faye McNamara and Dave Jackson who worked as supervisors on the excavations, Richard Wilson who wrote the architectural stone report, John Mattinson who wrote the coin report and Pat Bull the nail analysis. Joanne Wilkinson of Grampus Heritage Ltd. helped with post excavation analysis and the recording of the lead cames. Tim Padley of Tullie House Museum advised on identification of finds, ran workshops and wrote the metal report. Dot Broughton of Portable Antiquities also advised on finds and identified the spur in the metal report. Don O'Meara of North Pennines Archaeology wrote the environmental report and also ran workshops for the society. Member Marilyn Leech has been invaluable in helping with computing aspects of the report and in preparing figures and plates for publication. She also arranged the layout. Chris Cutts, chairman of WCAS, has helped with numerous computing problems. Pippa Murray drew the illustrations for the metalwork and tiles and prepared for publication the archive glass drawings provided by Rachel Tyson. Member Colin Mason proof read.

Rachel Tyson wrote the glass report and Lawrence Butler of Oxford University provided information on the grave slab, through Peter Ryder who advised us on stonework. Alison Goodall provided the note on the weight. Jennie Stopford kindly wrote the medieval tile report. Finally, Andrew Davison of English Heritage and Mark Brennand, County Archaeologist, must be thanked for their support and encouragement throughout.

Jan Walker

SUMMARY

This report seeks to consolidate our research so far into the history of the Abbey and archaeological investigations carried out from 2006–2010 within the scheduled monument area. The historical research, resistivity survey of 1976 and the magnetometry survey of 2006 were used as a basis for targeted excavation. This took place within the Abbey Precincts in the summers of 2008 and 2009, then two evaluation trenches were dug in the autumn of 2009 and spring of 2010, followed by three more evaluation trenches at Kiln Close field, Applegarth, adjoining the church land, and a final excavation in the summer of 2010.

The excavations of the early twentieth century were also re-examined. These excavations, together with our own findings through magnetometry, excavation and archival research, have enabled us to revisit the plan of the Abbey produced in 1925 and make significant alterations, which are discussed. The excavations and the archival research have also enabled us to reconstruct the history and archaeology of the Abbey since the Dissolution. The finds have added appreciably to our awareness of the Abbey, its life and its importance.

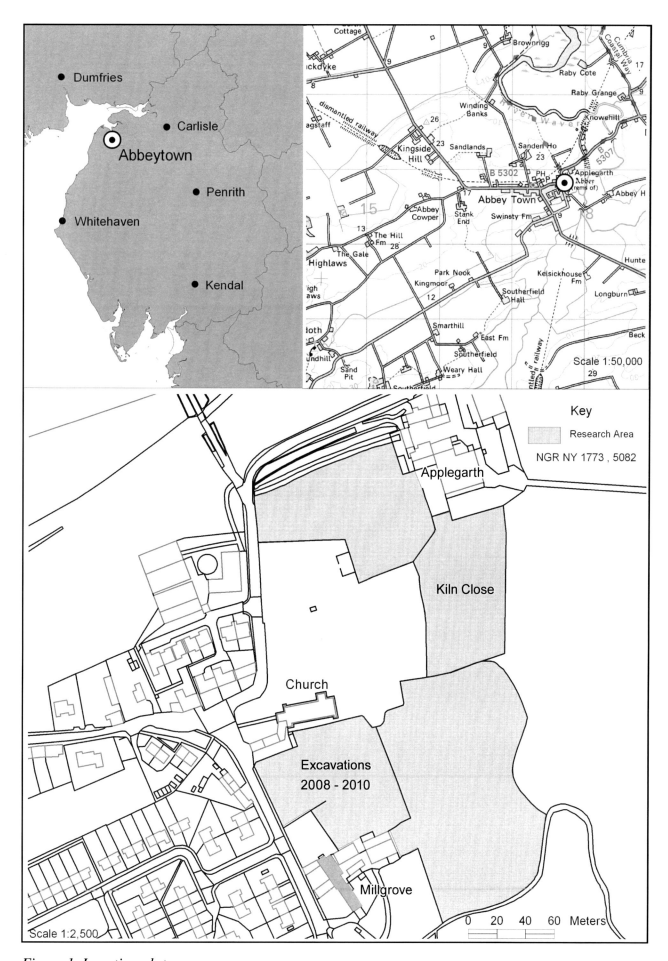

Figure 1: Location plots

Frontispiece: St. Mary's Abbey, western porch

The West Cumbria Archaeology Society was established in the year 2000 with the aim of being active in both fieldwork and research. The Society's interest is in practical archaeology and in giving members of the community the opportunity to handle artefacts, use archival material and undertake field walking and geophysical surveys, as well as excavation. The Society has long had an interest in St. Mary's Abbey. After initial research it was decided to undertake a magnetometry survey in 2006. Immediately before the survey the church was the victim of arson, and the roof of the church was totally destroyed with considerable damage to the interior. The magnetometry survey was opportune and received considerable interest from the village of Abbeytown. As a result of the survey the decision was made to excavate. A trench was excavated in the summer of 2008 which proved the potential of the site and demonstrated that the Society had the capacity to continue the work in terms of labour and professional support. Consequently an application was made successfully to the Heritage Lottery Fund for a community excavation to run over the next three years and for the subsequent analysis of the results and report. English Heritage supported permission to excavate on a scheduled monument which was readily granted by the Department of Culture, Media and Sport.

St. Mary's Abbey, Holme Cultram, Abbeytown is situated on an esker just south of the Solway Firth surrounded by marshes and beside the River Waver. The buildings are set below the east end of the ridge on its south side just out of sight of the mouth of the Solway Firth but would, from the inland aspect, have been seen from many miles around. It is not on the highest point which might seem to be the most logical place, but this may be because it is sited on a line of springs for water supply and near the river for ease of transport. The surrounding marsh and mosses of the Solway Plain make it a remote and inhospitable place, typical for a Cistercian Abbey.

THE HISTORICAL BACKGROUND
Pat Bull and Kate Rennicks

Toponymy
The name Holme Cultram varies in spelling; 'Holm' and 'Holme' are widely used; the latter spelling is currently in favour in the parish and is used throughout this report. 'Holme' originates from the Old Norse 'holmr' and means land almost surrounded by water, still an accurate description of the site. Cultram or Culteram is probably derived from the Latin, meaning 'to cultivate', i.e. ploughed land (Armstrong, ed., 1950). There is a hint that religious occupation at Holme Cultram may be very early; the 'Recapitulation' appended to the History by Symeon of Durham (854AD) lists places belonging to the bishopric of Lindisfarne. After "Lugubalia that is Luel now called Carleil", Symeon mentions a mansion called Culterham (Symeonis Dunelmensis, 1868, 67–68). Melrose, the founder Abbey of Holme Cultram, was also in the bishopric of Lindisfarne.

Remains of the Abbey's impact on the landscape can be seen in the area's modern place names. They include 'Applegarth', the monastic orchards; Abbey Cowper or 'Cow-byre'; the 'Stank' (an old Cumbrian name) denoting an area of wetland to the west of the present village, the fish ponds; and 'Swinsty', the site of the pig pens.

Historical Sources
There are three extant cartularies, one at Carlisle and two held at the British Library *(Jamroziak, 2008, 28)*. Possibly the most accessible modern copy is the *'Register and Records of Holm Cultram'* by Francis Grainger and W. G. Collingwood, published for the Cumberland and Westmorland Antiquarian and Archaeological Society in 1929. This draws upon the Carlisle copy and includes additions from the other two *(ibid.)*. This charter evidence proves useful in

corroborating some of the finds during excavation and also in examining the Abbey's sphere of influence, economic position and relations with the local area. Gilbanks' account of 1899 is also useful for its reproduction of church warden's records and engravings and particularly in tracing the later life of the buildings.

The Wider Monastic Landscape and Structures

The length of the original Abbey church is recorded at 279ft in length and 135ft (approximately 85m by 41m) at greatest width (Gilbanks, 1899, 29). The appearance of the parish church today is a result of extensive remodelling and reconstruction in 1730 when a structure was formed using six of the original nine bays of the nave arcade (Harrison, 2004).

Few ancillary buildings remain although there were nearby cottages shown on the first edition Ordnance Survey map (now demolished) and it is possible that these were remnants of the monastic structures. Millgrove, the range of buildings to the south west of the Abbey, is now a farmhouse and has been investigated by Peter Ryder (historic building consultant) and by Nina Jennings (notes in CRO). A medieval stone drain still runs under this building and can be seen in the cellar (Ryder, 2010). The northern part of the building in particular shows medieval features. It has traditionally been interpreted as the infirmary, rebuilt in 1472 but it could equally well be the lodgings for the Abbot and his guests. The present kitchen and tearoom adjacent to the Abbey church has monastic origins and still has a decorative fireplace incorporating the Chambers' arms in the upstairs room, now used as the parish office.

Much of the present external embellishment of the front of the Abbey was completed in the later 15th and early-16th century by Abbot Robert Chambers (c1489–1519). Chambers' building programme included the ground floor of the existing west porch which bears his coat of arms and an inscription giving the date MDVII (1507). In 1927 the porch still bore the feet and an inscription on a statue. Fragments of his tomb are now embedded in the wall of the present ambulatory. This tomb is a particularly interesting example of late Cistercian work showing the Abbot on his throne with a bishop's crozier, surrounded by his monks. As the number of the monks depicted tallies with the record of those who remained in the monastery at the time it is possible that they might have been identifiable when the sculptures were done and before their faces were destroyed by later reformers.

The lands within the 'Holm' included seven granges with a great barn at The Old Grange (Sandenhouse Grange), a barn and dovecote at Raby and a barn at Skinburgh. There were eight chapels and these are listed as St. John's at Skinburness, St. Roche near Goodyhills; St. Cuthbert's at Chapel Hill, New Cowper (still occupied at the Dissolution and recorded as being pulled down by 1688), Wolsty Chapel (a chapel is mentioned in the record of the dismantling of the castle by the Chambers family in 1636); St. Christian's at Sandenhouse (desecrated before the Dissolution); St. Thomas's (demolished before 1645 and possibly the infirmary chapel), and St. John's at Newton Arlosh licensed in 1304 and still with 'furniture' in 1535 but which is described as having been decayed for 20 years in 1603 (Grainger and Collingwood 1929, 164–167). Tracing the location of these granges and chapels will be a topic of future study.

The original boundary of the Abbey is recorded in the charters (Grainger and Collingwood 1929, 91; CRO PR/122/190). The boundary essentially remained the same through to the Dissolution and it is still followed by the parish boundaries. It is possible to trace much of the boundary from Angerton on the Wampool to the Solway near Mawbray. Grainger and Collingwood (1929, 121) record the traditional riding of the stretch between Kirkbride and the parish of Holme every seven years in 1927. An extant ditch and bank marking the eastern boundary of the monastic land, called Monk's Dyke, is now the parish boundary between Kirkbride and the parish of Holme Waver East and can still be seen beside a part of the Cumbrian Coastal Path. There is also part of a ditch and bank just north of the existing graveyard at Holme Cultram and bordering Applegarth Farm (Fig. 3). It is a substantial earthwork and can be seen continuing to the west. Holme Cultram Abbey received a licence to fortify its precinct in 1304 (Goodman, 1989, 258) and it is intended to trace this feature in future work.

It is likely that the earliest monastic buildings were of wooden construction (Grainger and Collingwood, 1929, 125). This assertion has been supported by recent excavation and although it has not been possible to identify particular buildings, there is evidence of timber structures that pre-date stone ones. Historical evidence also supports this; the monks were granted permission to source building material in Inglewood Forest in the foundation charter (Grainger and Collingwood, 1929, 35, 57). Certainly the red sandstone of which the Abbey is constructed is anomalous to the local glacial geology, as the only readily available local stone is glacier-borne boulders. Excavations (discussed later) show that the earliest foundations consisted of these boulders. Ferguson records the discovery of chipped red sandstone on the banks of the River Waver at its closest point to the Abbey (Ferguson, 1874, 273). It is therefore reasonable to assume that construction material for the Abbey was transported to the site by boat and dressed locally. As to its source, similar sandstone can be found in Southern Scotland, across the Solway and locally to Aspatria.

Establishment

The founding of Holme Cultram Abbey is set in the turbulent history of the politics between Scotland and England. William II added Cumberland to his Norman kingdom in 1092 and it remained in English hands until 1136. Henry 1 strengthened English influence in the North by founding the Augustinian Priory of St. Mary in Carlisle and created the diocese of Carlisle in 1133. When Henry I died in 1136, David I of Scotland took advantage of the situation to reclaim Carlisle and expand into the northern borders. His son, Prince Henry, founded Holme Cultram Abbey in 1150. The tutor to Prince Henry was Aelred of Rievaulx, Master of the Household of King David before he became a Cistercian monk. Probably it was his influence that led to the foundation of Melrose and its daughter houses, Holme Cultram amongst them, as Cistercian monasteries. The Abbey's foundation charter is missing and only survives as quoted fragments, but the date of the foundation is mentioned as 1150 in the Chronicles of Melrose and quoted in the register of the Priory of Wetherall. In 1157 Henry II succeeded the English throne and forced the then King of Scotland, Malcolm IV, to surrender the northern counties to England. The cartulary provides a copy of royal charter of 1158, in which Henry II, *"takes into his protection the abbey of Holmecoltran and grants the whole island of Holme Coltran and Rabi by the right bounds; also timber in Englewode forest for buildings, etc. and pasture for pigs without [paying] pannage, and bark from the trees they fell"*. This endowment was later confirmed by Richard I, John I, Henry III, and Edward I (Grainger and Collingwood, 1929, 206–226).

It is material that the fragments of the foundation charter describe the land as 'the island of holm'. The location of the Abbey is on higher ground than the surrounding land and still today, in

3

periods of wet weather, the land appears as an island. Although any building on this site would clearly stand out in the landscape, it is not clear why this particular piece of land was considered special enough to be endowed to a religious house. However, the siting does lend support to the possibility of an early Christian site already in existence (Symeonis Dunelmensis, 1868, p.67–68). The charter evidence suggests that the land was marginal and of poor agricultural value, so it could be argued that the endowment, although altruistic, was self-serving in that the land in itself was not considered to have economic worth. On the other hand, in Western Europe in the 10th and 11th centuries, there was widespread dissatisfaction with the monastic observance of the Benedictines and Cluniacs. This manifested itself in a yearning to return to the ideal of the desert fathers, particularly championed by the Cistercians who sought the isolation provided by mountains, forests, marshes and wastelands (Aston 2000, 79) and it is possible that the location of Holme Cultram is indicative of this behaviour.

Royal Patronage and Influence

It is clear that during the early years of its foundation, Holme Cultram Abbey enjoyed a position of some influence. The first Abbot, Everard, was a noted academic and author of several hagiographies including the lives of Saints Waldeve, Abbot of Melrose, Cumen and Adamnan. He is recorded as having attended the coronation of Richard I, the Lionheart, witnessed several charters, and was a friend of Christian, Bishop of Whithorn who later retired and was interred at Holme Cultram (Fordun, Scoticron, cited in Grainger and Collingwood, 1929, 120).

Later Abbots, although never mitred, can be traced at various times during the 12th and 13th centuries, witnessing charters and sitting in judgement in different parts of both England and Scotland. They were also regularly granted permission and funds to undertake the journey to Citeaux in Burgundy for the Chapter General (Cal Close Rolls 13 Ed II Westminster: see Grainger and Collingwood, 1929, 141 and Cal Close Rolls 8 Ed III cited in *ibid*. 144). One Abbot, Gilbert (1233–37) died at Canterbury on his way back from the Chapter General. (Grainger and Collingwood, 1929, 134).

Through its monastic life, Holme Cultram enjoyed royal patronage. Robert the Bruce (father of King Robert I of Scotland) was buried there in 1294 (his grave slab is located in the present day ambulatory). The Abbey's port of Skinburness was home to the English fleet in 1300 for the siege of Caerlaverock and was used to import supplies for the army in the campaigns against the Scots by Edward 1 (1272–1307).

Edward I used the Abbey as a base for his Scottish campaigns of 1299 and in July 1307 was travelling to Holme Cultram at the time of his death on Burgh Marsh (Summerson 2011, 36). His entrails are alleged to be buried locally and subsequently the Abbey tried, rather unsuccessfully, to style itself as a burial place of the King (Jamroziak, 2008, 34). There are a number of petitions from the Abbey claiming restitution for goods supplied to both Edward I and II.

Importance of Position – A Frontier Abbey

In the 1150s the border people were closely connected socially and economically, and many landowners (including the Abbey) held estates on both sides of the Solway. *'This great abbey, which overshadowed in riches and influence the rest of the religious houses in Cumberland and Westmorland, had many friends and benefactors on both sides of the Border before rupture with Scotland in 1296. Endowments were freely lavished upon it by landowners, large and small, in various parts of the two counties'* (Wilson, ed., 1905, 166–73). This is perhaps a reflection of its location and the fact that the Solway is likely to have formed more of a natural highway than the land routes.

Despite being situated on English controlled soil, Holme Cultram continued to defer spiritual authority to its mother house at Melrose. The Abbey had significant landholdings on the Scottish side of the Solway but this did not prevent frequent Scottish raiding. In February 1216, Alexander II of Scotland raided Cumberland and pillaged the Abbey, going so far as to remove the bed covering from a sick monk in the Infirmary. In 1235, the lay brothers were granted licence to bear arms to protect their granges and Pope Innocent (although which Innocent is not clear) issued a threat of excommunication for any person that *'troubled the monks'* (Grainger and Collingwood, 1929, 96–102). Their willingness to defend their lands is demonstrated at the grange church of Newton Arlosh, where the church appears as more of a fortified keep than a religious house, and also at the fortified tower at Wolsty (now demolished), specifically designed as a secure place to keep the monastic records.

These attacks gave rise to a need to rebuild and the charters record that a quarry was provided for the Abbey sometime between 1210 and 1223 at the place known as 'Sandwith in Aspatric'. This may be Westnewton Quarry, one mile north of Aspatria (Grainger and Collingwood, 1929, 23; Wilson ed., 1905 162–173; Dugdale, 1817–30, 78). Woods were also granted for building material (Grainger and Collingwood, 1929, 35, 57). In 1319 some of the monks dispersed *'until the house of Holmcoltram be released from its oppression'* (Cal Close Rolls 13 Edward II, cited in Grainger and Collingwood, 1929, 141). In 1428 the Pope granted indulgences to penitents visiting the Abbey church who gave alms for its repair (Grainger and Collingwood, 1929, 149). During the 14th century the Abbey's fortunes succumbed to the famines, plagues,

cattle murrain and continuing Scottish raids. The foundation became so destitute they petitioned the Crown to be excused dues and taxes, pleading poverty (Wilson, ed., 1905, 164). Despite this the Abbots were still involved in the affairs of state and appear as witnesses in several charters.

By the 13th and 14th century, charters seem to show a shift away from Scottish roots to a more Southern looking perspective, no doubt as a consequence of the raiding. However, it is clear that above all, the Abbey was primarily local in its outlook and sustained by a number of Cumbrian benefactors. Indeed, Jamroziak (2008, 35–6) suggests that without the wars Holme Cultram would have continued to successfully span and bridge the border.

To consider Holme Cultram as a border foundation would be to ignore its proximity to the sea and there is some historical evidence to suggest that the Abbey was part of a wider Irish Sea community. This is perhaps best illustrated in its ties with the controversial figure of John de Courcy in the 12th century. De Courcy was a Norman knight who arrived in Ireland 1176, was expelled in 1204 and during that time is credited with the conquest of the kingdom of Ulaid (modern north east Ulster). His conquests were opportunistic and carried out without the permission of the crown, hence his later expulsion, yet for over a quarter of a century, he ruled in the manner of a king in north-east Ireland.

The story of de Courcy's conquest in Ulster has been well documented elsewhere, but it is worth briefly recounting some of it in order to give some reasoning for the establishment of Holme Cultram's daughter house some 70 miles across the Irish Sea. His first posting to Ireland was to the garrison at Dublin but within some months, he grew dissatisfied with the inactivity of his commander and drew together a band of

300 men to set off on conquest. Interestingly though, de Courcy marched straight through swathes of unconquered territory and headed for Down (now Downpatrick), capital of the kingdom of Ulaid, the territory of the far north east of Ulster, bordering the Irish Sea. Duffy (1995) demonstrated that although traditionally described as having hailed from Somerset, de Courcy had important connections with Cumbria through his maternal relatives. Neither his territorial choice nor his marriage to Affreca, daughter of Godred II, King of Man, in around 1180 were accidental and are suggestive of an attempt to consolidate an Irish Sea empire.

This is nowhere more obvious than in the religious endowments of the de Courcys. Holme Cultram's involvement in what has become known as 'the first Ulster plantation' is first seen in 1183 when Everard, the first Abbot, is recorded as a witness on a charter for the establishment of St. Thomas the Martyr's priory at Toberglory, Downpatrick and made it a cell of St. Mary's, Carlisle (Duffy, 1995, 9). This was one of several establishments in which the mother house was Cumbrian, drawing the two sides of the Irish Sea closer and with the Isle of Man acting as a bridging point. Some ten years later following the death of Everard, Affreca made a foundation at Grey Abbey and set this up as a daughter house of Holme Cultram (Harrison, 2002, 115–116).

Despite John de Courcy's later imprisonment for his separatist tendencies, Holme Cultram maintained an Irish Sea relationship. Affreca's father Godred II had already granted the Abbey freedom from tolls in the Isle of Man and this relationship was perpetuated by two of his successors (Grainger and Collingwood, 1929, 94–5). In addition, one of the Abbey's chief benefactors in the 13th century was the de Rumilly family, relations of John de Courcy on his maternal side (Duffy, 1995, 10). There is also speculation that the third Abbot of Holme

Cultram, one William de Courcy was the son (or at least relative) of John and Affreca, although this cannot be substantiated (Gilbanks, 1900, 39). All these interconnected threads point to the location of Holme Cultram being significant. The Abbey may have been on the periphery of both English and Scottish soil but there are grounds to suggest that its position on the Irish Sea was key to its continuation as a viable foundation despite the privations suffered as a consequence of the Anglo-Scottish wars.

Trade and Economy

Although the Abbey clearly suffered through raiding, it used its location to strategic advantage and the charters show that it maximized its trading capability to great effect (see below for archaeological evidence of trading links). The trade and economy of the monastic landscape is the subject of on-going study and further excavation is anticipated to understand the relationship of the monastery with the wider world.

By 1175, the monastery had five granges (Grainger and Collingwood, 1929, 122) and was renowned for producing some of the purest salt in the country. In 1301, the Abbey was granted right to a free burgh on the coast at Skinburness, a weekly market on Thursday and a yearly fair of 17 days' duration (Grainger and Collingwood, 1929, 95-96). The greater part of the borough of Skinburness was swept away by the sea in 1305 and privileges were consequently transferred to Newton Arlosh as compensation and again, locating the port will be the subject of future study. The charters also suggest that the Abbey had a policy of securing land in which they had trading markets, such as Carlisle and Hartlepool, through which it exported wool. The wool was considered of an inferior quality (Grainger and Collingwood, 1929, 114). They also held land in Newcastle, and Boston for the purpose of attending the annual fair (*ibid.* 38-39, 87-88 & 90-91). They were granted and willed parcels of land in many other areas including what is now Dumfries and Galloway.

Clearly, the Abbey was successful in its business ventures given that at the Dissolution, it was recorded as having seven granges and chapels. In 1535 *the Valor Ecclesiasticus,* cited in Hutchinson (1794, 343) gives the Abbey's income as £477.19s3½d and the value of its possessions as £117.3s9d. At the Dissolution, it was the wealthiest monastery in Cumberland.

Later Monastic Life and Post Monastic Decline

In the later years of Holme Cultram, there are some entries in the charters that give insight into the flavour of local life in the area. Spiritual laxity and inappropriate mixing with the extra mural community appear to have been prevalent. In 1472, there was a vacancy at Holme Cultram, and Abbot Richard of Melrose visited the house to preside at the election of a new abbot. Who the Abbot elected was we do not know, but Richard of Melrose as superior caused a code of injunctions to be read in the chapter house on November 30, 1472. In this he ordered the monks to celebrate the daily and nightly offices of the Blessed Virgin and the canonical hours; to receive the Eucharist, if priests, four times a week and if in lower orders twice at least in the fortnight; to study the Scriptures as the surest refuge in all troubles; to allow no monk out of bounds alone; to permit no women within the precincts; to provide a schoolmaster for the younger brethren; to rebuild the infirmary and to supply the inner doors of the monastery with locks to keep out unwelcome visitors; and finally, as monks must not be mixed up with secular affairs, to forbid any of them, and especially brother John Ribtoun, to be bailiff or forester or otherwise engage in worldly business (according to the *Liber S. Marie de Melrose,* i, 596–9, cited in Wilson, ed., 1905, 65 and cited in Grainger and Collingwood, 1929, 149).

These faults were rectified through what seem to have been years of prosperity and construction during the abbacy of Robert Chambers, but this was not to last. The sources contain an account of the death of Abbot Matthew Deveys in which a monk, Gawain Borrodaile, was accused of poisoning him and was imprisoned at Furness Abbey for his crime. The testimonies of the monks during the trial are extensively recorded (Gilbanks, 1900, 91-97) and provide an insight into local politics, engaging the abbots of several Cumbrian monasteries and hinting that Holme Cultram no longer enjoyed quite the power and patronage that it once did.

The Abbey was meanwhile assessed by Thomas Cromwell, who appears to have employed a spy called Thomas Graym the Cellarer to list the misdeeds of Abbot Thomas Carter, claiming that *'he has brought women into the monastery to dine and sup. Has sold without licence £100 of plate. Has used the seal against our profit. Has given to the Abbot of Byland a salt of gold and silver, value 20 marks. Has sold our jewels of our kirk. Has let the demesne lands against the King's injunction'.* Although it is likely that Graym was Cromwell's spy, Abbot Thomas Carter was certainly involved in the Pilgrimage of Grace in 1536–7 and does appear to have sold the church plate to finance the rebellion (Gilbanks, 1900, 98–105). He was pardoned for his part in the revolt but the following year was involved when the Duke of Norfolk besieged Carlisle, after which no trace of him has been found. As other leaders were hung drawn and quartered perhaps he suffered this fate or maybe he discreetly disappeared (Wilson, ed., 1905). The final Abbot was Gawain Borrodaile of poisoning fame who appears to have been appointed specifically to surrender the monastery (Gilbanks, 1990, 106–111). The deed of surrender was signed by the Abbot and twenty-four monks on March 6th, 1538. Borrodaile continued in spiritual charge of the lordship of Holmcultram

7

and had *"for his logyng ' with which he was 'ryght well contentyd, the chambre that he was in before he was abbot, then called the selleras chambre, and the chambre at the stayr hed adjoynyng to the same.'* (Wilson, ed. 1905, 162–173, URL http://www.british-history.ac).

The church itself was left standing, after a petition by the inhabitants to Cromwell in 1538 (Grainger and Collingwood, 1929, 153–163). However, most of the outlying buildings at the Abbey were dismantled and anything valuable sold or stolen so that by 1561 there was *"not remaining within the precinct of the late monastery neyther bell, yron, glass (etc.) upon anye house but one chamber..........but there are certain old walles yet standing as well of the church as of other houses about the same which we have appoynted to.....sell to the Queen's Majesty's use after viijd everie load of stone"* (Grainger and Collingwood, 1929, 158).

It seems probable that some of the east range remained, as arches were reported to still be there in the 17th century (J Denton Manuscript 1687–1688). There is a report for March 1665 that stones were *"led out of old walls by Francis Threlkeld"* and others were digging for Rob Farish who when charged with this said he *"would take no stop at anie man"* (Grainger, 1921, 96–129). Many of the surrounding farm buildings incorporate examples of carved stones and a list with drawings was made in 1925 and lodged at Tullie House Museum, Carlisle.

Eventually the only complete buildings left were the church nave, the possible ex-abbots' lodgings called the "celleras", the old infirmary and the mill. From 1555-1580 John Estwicke, the rector neglected both his responsibilities and the fabric of the building (Wilson, ed., 1905). In 1600 the structure had deteriorated so much the steeple fell bringing down part of the chancel. For the next two years much lead, wood and stone was carried away (Grainger, 1921, 112). In 1553, on the death of Gawain Borrodaile, Queen Mary granted the rectory of Holme Cultram, and chapel and church of Newton Arlosh to the University of Oxford. The University of Oxford commissioned a new chancel, but in 1604 the roof of the church was set on fire and burnt down in three hours. Chris Harding, the priests' servant, had carried a live coal up into the roof to light a candle to search for a chisel (Ashworth, 1887).

The decay continued so that by 1630 the Bishop of Carlisle reported that it was a "great ruin" (Grainger and Collingwood, 1929, 179).

In 1640 Peter Senhouse, steward, complained of *'swine wourting in the graveyard'* (Ashworth, 1867). Sporadic repairs were made and a tax raised for this purpose in 1650 (Grainger, 1903, 172-213). In 1688 the last of the usable stone was sold (Denton, 1687-1688). In 1703, Bishop Nicolson noted that it was raining into the church and described how 15 years earlier, the lead had been taken from the south aisle to cover the arches of the north, and consequently, only the body of the church was still standing (Martindale, 1913). Despite the Bishop's visit, it took until 1730 for proper repairs to be made. Even so the church remained very damp and it continued in decline until 1882 when the church was restored. The fire of 2006 destroyed the remaining old beams, said to be from the 12th century *(ibid.)* and the building is now reroofed.

The Archaeological Background
Jan Walker

Over the years Holme Cultram has been extensively robbed for its prime quality building stone. This is apparent in a walk around Abbeytown; many of the houses incorporate worked stone which very probably comes from the Abbey. The written records also attest to this.

In addition, the written records show the church was in poor repair and that the monastic stone was used to repair the church. Around 1688 lead was taken from one aisle to repair the other (Bishop Nicolson, visitation 1703); also at this date there are records of building stone being removed (Grainger, 1921). In 1727–1765, under the Chancellorship of Chancellor Waugh, repairs were carried out on the church which involved the removal of the side aisles and part of the chancel.

No recorded archaeological excavation took place in the Abbey grounds until the 1870s, when Mr Charles Ferguson obtained funding from the CWAAS and, with the permission of the then vicar, Mr Ashworth, began an investigation to ascertain the extent of the aisles. With the help of Mr Steel of Southerfield, who supervised the excavations, a trench was dug from the church on the north side, *'about two feet (61cm) from the north east corner of the buttress of the present church'* (Ferguson, 1874, 263-273). Approximately two feet (61cm) down they encountered two courses of worked stone six feet (1·83m) thick, which they interpreted as the inner wall of the aisle. The dimensions of the nave arcade are given as 32 feet (9·76m) from centre to centre, from the centre to the inside of the aisle wall as 13 feet 2 inches (4·02m). A portion of the transept walls was also uncovered, and they recorded that the walls were coloured.

Ferguson stated (Ferguson, 1874, 263-273) that the whole of the east end of the church was filled with debris from the fall of the tower, which demolished the choir and transepts, and that remains of floor tiles were sometimes seen in this area.

Unfortunately no archaeological records survive of these excavations; there is a reconstructed plan showing the transept walls, but the exact position of the trenches is not marked.

In the spring of 1906, Mrs T.H. Hodgson and her husband recorded remains exposed during alterations being made at the church (Hodgson, 1907, 262-268). Foundations of pillars had been uncovered in the churchyard, together with a doorway in line with the northern row of pillars, 76 feet (23·1m) from the eastern end of the present church. Detailed measurements of the doorway and wall were taken, together with photographs. On the south side of the walls running east and west of the doorway in what would have been the choir, a well was recorded next to the door together with some cylindrical fragments of shaft.

In front of the doorway, to the south and southwest an area of floor tiles *in situ* was revealed. This was carefully drawn and recorded by the Hodgsons. To the north of the doorway more floor tiles were uncovered, which were removed and placed in the porch of the church. Part of a stone figure was also uncovered and photographed, then removed to the porch of the church. Martindale (1913, 244-251) stated that the church was *'undoubtedly rebuilt and extended in the Early English period'*. He suggested there were also alterations to the north pier of the crossing, possibly dating to the 1600 Mandeville rebuild, though he suggested that they looked later 17th century in date.

The Hodgsons' trench of 1906 (Fig. 2, Pl. 16) is still clearly visible in the eastern end of the churchyard. It is very overgrown with raspberry canes and brambles obscuring the sides. The West Cumbria Archaeological Society cleared the trench of undergrowth in 2009, and uncovered a sufficient number of tiles to establish that they were still *in situ*. They then covered the tiles with protective material and backfilled over them to protect them from frost. They also accurately measured and plotted the doorway with a total station (Pl. 17).

Work in 1906 was also recorded by the Rector, the Revd W. Baxter, and Mr C. Forster of the British Archaeological Association. The Revd Baxter published a note of the discoveries in their journal (Baxter, 1907, 126-130) with plans and drawings by Mr C. Forster. Baxter states their aim was to determine the extreme eastern wall of the original Abbey church. They thought they found this following the line of the old thorn hedge which forms the eastern boundary, presumably of the churchyard. At the south eastern end of this wall there was a buttress foundation. At the south eastern corner stone mullions were found embedded in clay. These were interpreted as part of the window which fell in after gales in

March 1579 (Grainger and Collingwood, 1929, 176).

The other side of the hedge was also investigated but yielded no stonework, only human bones, leading them to conclude this was the monastic burial ground.

On the south side, the existing boundary hedge runs close to the south side of the transept and excavation here revealed large blocks of stone. The West Cumbria Archaeological Society with Grampus Heritage Ltd. located and re-excavated this trench on the side of the graveyard in late 2010 (it was not possible to excavate outside the graveyard because it was within the scheduled monument area and permission had not been

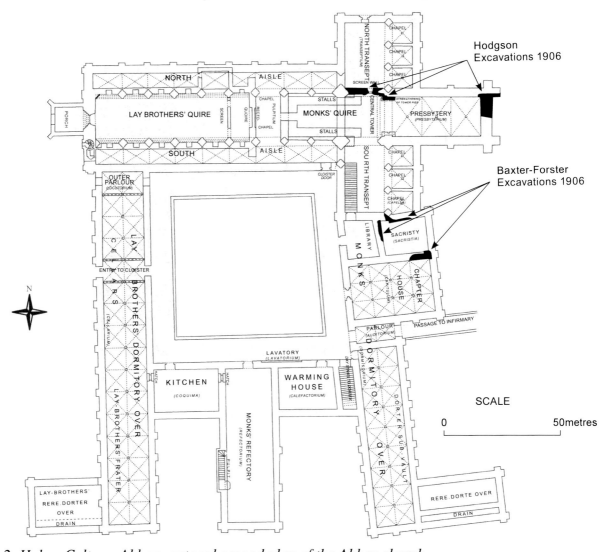

Figure 2: Holme Cultram Abbey; restored ground plan of the Abbey church and conventual buildings showing earlier excavations 1925 (Martindale, 1925)

10

sought). They located and recorded the stones mentioned and re-plotted them using a total station (Fig. 19, Pl. 18). The foundations were interpreted as a possible sacristy, beyond the transept with an entrance from the cloister walk, or a possible chapel, by Baxter (1907, 126-130).

Well within the scheduled area and therefore not re-excavated and plotted by WCAS was another trench, 26 feet (7·93m) further south, where more large foundation stones forming the outer wall of a building were found. This was interpreted as a possible chapter house by Baxter (1907). Martindale (1913, 244-251) stated the distance was 27 feet (8.23m) from the south wall of the transept, and concluded the chapter house was rectangular and therefore probably Norman and part of the original foundation. He compared this to Easby, and also drew a parallel with the wheel stairs at Easby in the north wall of the chapter house, remains of which he reported were discovered at Holme Cultram.

Based on the excavation at the turn of the century Martindale produced a reconstructed plan of the church and monastic layout. It is likely the original measurements were made using chains, and were taken from the core of the walls rather than from the facing stones, leading to some inaccuracy, which when projected led to the misalignment illustrated in Fig. 2. The re-excavation of the old sites by WCAS rectified the problem; with modern surveying equipment we were able to record the true alignment of the walls which resulted in a more conventional and likely layout (Fig. 46).

Martindale also recorded the block of buildings which were still standing to the south west of the church, c. 172 feet (52·46m) away. One of these had a date stone with 1664 and RF and FF which he linked to Robert Fayrish and his wife Frances. Various other architectural features he recorded indicate that these buildings were originally conventual buildings, including a large apartment or hall with a wide fireplace, or closet and a store. He suggested the buildings were originally the infirmary or the mill. *'Further west again'* he recorded a fragment of *'very ancient wall'* now incorporated into a barn (Martindale, 1913, 244-251). He described these buildings as cottages; by the description and photographs in the article he was without doubt referring to Millgrove Farm.

The map evidence for the Abbey buildings is sparse. The Gough map, dating to 1360 (CRO R1.08) marks the position of Holme Abbey, Holme Coltram, attesting to the importance of the Abbey by its inclusion. The Hodskinson and Donald map of 1774 (CRO R1.08) also shows the Abbey, and the area of the Stank, reputed to be the fishponds for the monastery. The Abbey is shown next on the Enclosure map of 1814, (CRO SRDWB/1) which shows outbuildings in the north west corner of the field where the excavations took place – this would be the present kitchens. Buildings are also shown on the western side of the field next to the road, possibly a small cottage. The 1818 map of Cumberland by Harrison and Fryer (CRO R 1.08) shows the Abbey as Abbey Holme; it is indistinct but it possibly shows a stream running north–south past the Abbey which may be water diverted from the River Waver. The 1821, 1822 Greenwood map (CRO R 1.08) shows the Abbey and the road system.

The 1850 tithe map (CRO DRC/8/93/2) shows the Abbey, but none of the immediate surrounding area – presumably because they did not pay tithes as church land.

The Ordnance Survey maps (CRO OS maps) are not particularly helpful, although the 1864 first edition (Fig. 3) shows the cottages on the west side of the field and a small building in the north west corner – the present kitchens as on the enclosure map. It also seems to show the mill buildings to the south, extending over the river. The line of cottages along the street to the Abbey all have wells; this may indicate a spring line and is in line with the well found at the south eastern corner of the present church found by the Hodgsons. The buildings in the north west corner of the field (present kitchens)

are still shown as in the field on the 1900 Ordnance Survey map, but no cottages on the western side of the field are shown. The situation is the same on the 1925 map. The 1976 version shows only that the area to the west has been built upon.

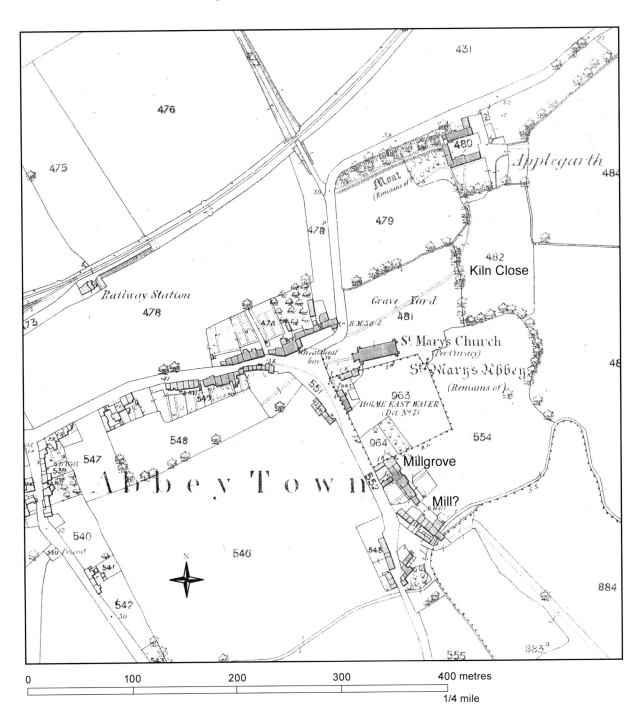

Figure 3: Holme Cultram Abbey; 1864 First Edition Ordnance Survey Map

12

Architechetural Background
St. Mary's Abbey, Holme Cultram
Jan Walker

The plan of the church is based on antiquarian and published sources (Martindale, 1913, 244-251; Harrison, 2007, 239-256). Access to the church to verify details at present is not possible due to renovation work following the 2006 fire.

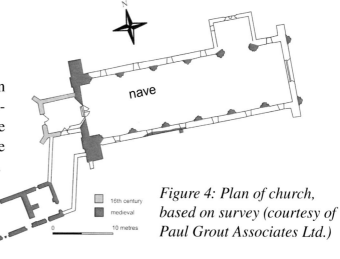

Figure 4: Plan of church, based on survey (courtesy of Paul Grout Associates Ltd.)

Plate 1: J. Cole's print c.1723 view of Holme Cultram Abbey from the north east: prior to the alterations in the 1730s

Plate 2: John Sumpton's drawing engraved by J. Cole, showing ruined buildings to the west with the nave reduced in size and the lost transepts and presbytery

Harrison (2007, 239-256) identifies four main rebuilding phases of the church. The first is the initial build, within twenty years of the foundation of the Abbey in 1150. Secondly is the reinforcement of the north east crossing pier in Early Gothic style to facilitate the building of the crossing and a tower. This took place in the thirteenth century. The next major alterations came with the Abbot Robert Chambers who rebuilt the main West porch in the sixteenth century. Finally the church was extensively remodelled in the 1730s. It is difficult to correlate these phases of development, when the church presumably had money to spend and expand, with the archaeological evidence, but the alterations to the refectory doorway discovered

Plate 3: Buck engraving of 1739 showing building cellaras with embattled parapets and remains of the transept arches

in 2008 may relate to Abbot Chamber's sixteenth century expansion, as might the works on the water supply which are evident in the 2010 excavations.

13

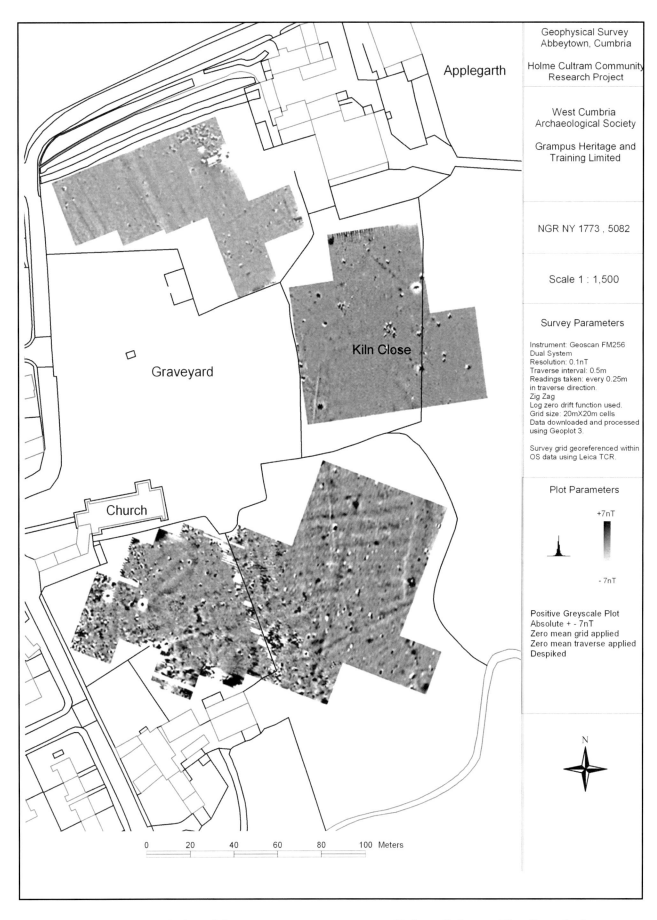

Figure 5: *Georeferenced plot of the magnetometer survey at Holme Cultram. The disturbed nature of the cloister area to the south of the church is distinctly different from the smooth, cleaner results gained to the east and north.*

14

GEOPHYSICAL SURVEY

Mark Graham

Background

During the summer of 2006, the West Cumbria Archaeological Society began a fieldwork project to undertake geophysical survey at Holme Cultram Abbey, Abbeytown (NY 177, 508). The survey aimed to increase understanding of the layout of the monastic complex and ascertain the extent of archaeological remains in the ground. This survey marked the beginning of a long-term research project, which took place between 2006 and 2011.

The first geophysical survey at Holme Cultram was conducted in 1976 by Phil Howard and Lyle Browning as part of an M.A. thesis for Bradford University, supervised by Arnold Aspinall. Mr Howard kindly shared the data from this early resistivity survey with the society and the results are reproduced (Fig. 6).

For the 2006 fieldwork, magnetometry was chosen in preference to resistivity due to the large area to be covered and the high resolution of results offered by the FM256 dual-system. This also allowed for a direct comparison of resistivity and magnetometry results on the same site (Figs. 6 & 7).

Permission to undertake the 2006 survey was kindly granted by Andrew Davison (English Heritage), Mr. McDonagh and Revd David Tembey. The survey was conducted using a Geoscan FM256 dual fluxgate gradiometer system, with data processed using Geoscan's Geoplot 3 software. All of the fieldwork was carried out by project volunteers with supervision and training provided by Grampus Heritage and Training Ltd. A grid of 20m x 20m cells was established on each site using hand tapes. The grid was deliberately placed on a different orientation to the church alignment to minimise any confusion between linear archaeological anomalies and survey traverse and grid lines. The survey was conducted at the following resolution: range 0·1nT, traverse interval 0·5m, readings taken every 0·25m in the traverse direction. The final results were georeferenced within Ordnance Survey map data using the total station (Leica TCR 307) to plot the grid position in association with field boundaries.

In 2011, a second geophysical survey was conducted in two fields to the north and north east of the church around the farm of Applegarth (Fig. 10). This survey was initiated following the identification of a field name of 'Kiln Close', marked on the 1864 edition of the Ordnance Survey map. The survey area also sought to investigate the land between an extant section of bank and ditch, marked on maps as 'moat' and the abbey. A plot of the whole result of the magnetometry survey is shown (Fig. 5).

Results

The result of the 1976 resistivity survey (Fig. 6), identified a number of archaeological anomalies. Of particular interest to our research was the suggested size of the cloister. Later excavation was to show that the 1976 survey accurately located the south western inner corner of the cloister. The resistivity survey also revealed evidence of the western range of buildings and a portion of the southern range. These are shown in the simplified interpretation plot (Fig. 6).

The magnetometer survey of the scheduled area to the south of the church produced markedly different results to the resistivity data. The magnetometry results are heavily disturbed and the data contains many iron spikes, resulting from ferrous objects in the ground. The internal cloister extent does not show well in the data, though a proposed external wall can be seen in the result. This perhaps represents the eastern and southern extent of these building ranges.

15

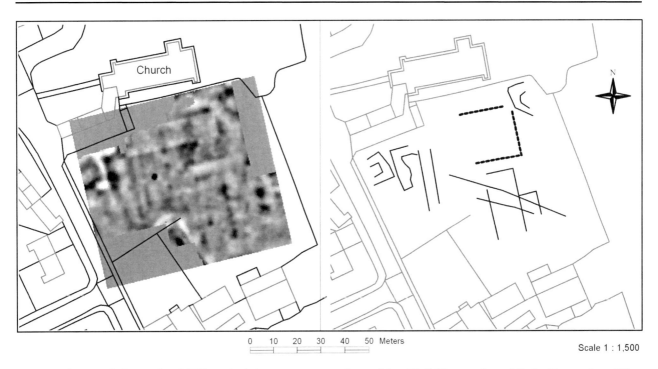

Figure 6: Result from the 1976 resistivity survey conducted by Phil Howard and Lyle Browning. The interpretation to the right shows the main identified archaeological anomalies including the cloister (dotted line) and elements of the southern and western ranges.

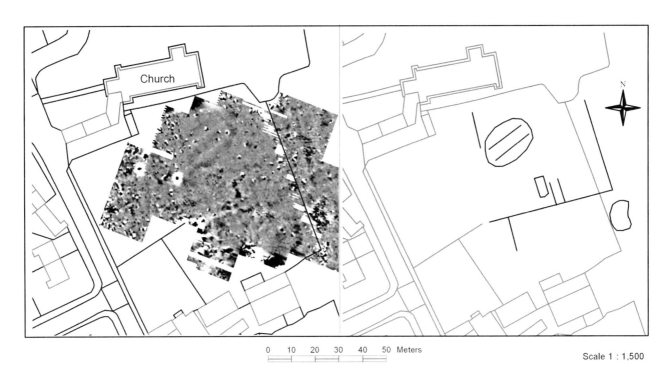

Figure 7: Result of the magnetometer survey in the cloister area to the south of the church. The data contains a number of iron spikes and areas of disturbance. The small rectilinear feature in the centre of the south range was the target for the first excavation in 2008.

The full result of the magnetometry survey is shown in Fig. 5. The heavy disturbance shown in the field to the south of the church differs from the 'cleaner' more uniform result gained to the east and north of the church. Fig. 7 offers a simple interpretation of some of the clearer anomalies in the cloister area, with the plot on the right of Fig. 7 showing the proposed outer limit of the east and south ranges. This plot also shows the small rectilinear feature, in the centre of the southern range, which was targeted in the first excavations in 2008. The strong black and white signal given by this feature suggested a thermoremnant anomaly, with the magnetic signal altered through burning activity rather than the presence of ferrous material.

The feature investigated by evaluation trench 2 in 2010, thought to be the possible site of an early church in the cloister garth, is also shown in this plot as parallel lines surrounded by a sub-circular feature (Fig. 7).

The land to the south east of the church, still within the scheduled area, shows a clear linear drainage pattern. This may obscure faint archaeological features to the south east of the church, though the topography and slope of the land in this area means that substantial buildings are unlikely to exist far beyond the eastern wall interpreted in Fig. 7.

The Kiln Close field survey, to the east of the graveyard, showed no clear archaeological anomalies while the survey between the graveyard and the bank and ditch to the north (Applegarth) showed only evidence of drainage and a possible track way. Three trenches were excavated to target anomalies to the west of Applegarth, though none of these produced any medieval material or any evidence of medieval activity.

Conclusions

With the benefit of excavation, it is now clear why the geophysical survey data was so disturbed in the southern fields. The heavy robbing of the site has resulted in deep, disturbed rubble deposits as well as large areas of dumped stone, with few walls or foundations remaining. Geophysical survey at the site proved to be a useful first step in understanding the extent of archaeological remains and provided a clear target for the first phase of excavation in 2008. More detailed interpretation of the geophysical data is problematic without the benefit of excavation. The results were not as clear as hoped and wall lines can only be interpreted with a low level of confidence, given the heavy robbing and spreads of resulting rubble which cover the site.

The results of both the resistivity and magnetometry surveys show wall lines which are parallel and perpendicular to the surviving church. The current field boundary which sub-divides the scheduled area to the south of the church does not form a right angle with the church alignment, leading Martindale (1912) on his plan (Fig. 2) to conclude that the eastern range also ran at this alignment and that the cloister garth was not square (or rectilinear) as would be usual in a Cistercian house. The wall lines shown in the geophysical data, and subsequent excavations, show that this field boundary does not follow the alignment of the east range.

Despite the difficulty in interpreting the results to the south of the church, the technique of magnetometry does show a clear distinction between archaeological activity and 'sterile areas'. It is hoped that a further programme of survey may detect further activity associated with the monastery including the continuation of the moat to the north and west.

17

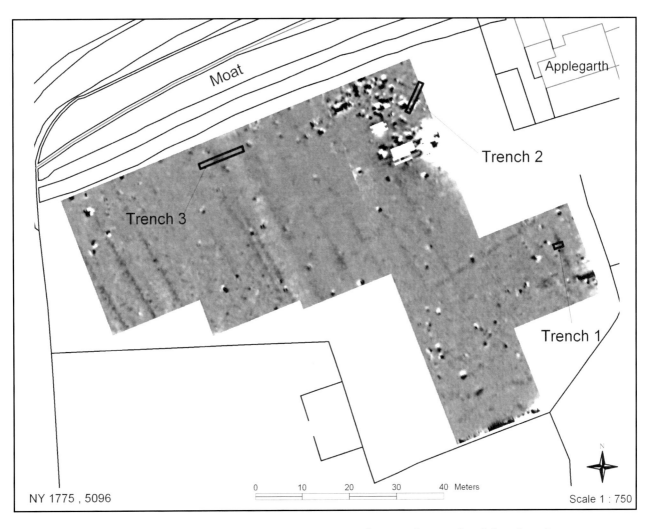

Figure 8: The 2011 trenches over the Applegarth survey data to the north of the church

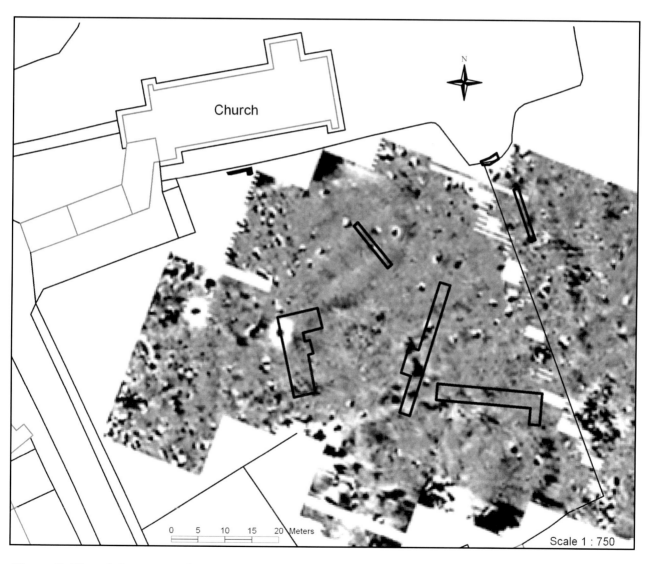

Figure 9: Trench locations shown over the magnetometry data (trench numbers as in Figure 10)

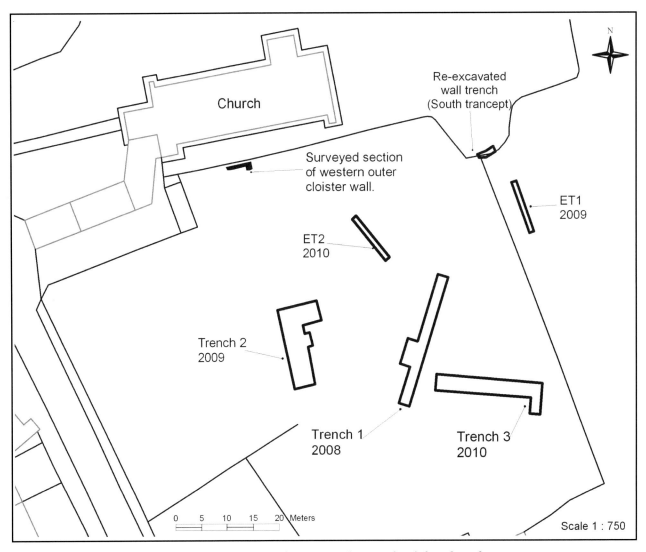

Figure 10: Trench locations in main research area to the south of the church

THE EXCAVATIONS

Mark Graham and Jan Walker

All context numbers are in brackets; context numbers shown on the figures are in italics.

THE 2008 EXCAVATION

The magnetometry survey seemed to highlight the possible southern side of the cloister, and a trench was situated to investigate this and two putative buildings. The field is under pasture and shows evidence of earthworks and areas of disturbance, and these were also taken into account. A project design, full research design and application for scheduled monument consent to excavate was prepared and submitted to the Department of Culture, Media and Sport following discussions with English Heritage in the early summer of 2008. Subsequently consent was granted and the church landowners gave their permission for a small scale excavation. The six week excavation took place in September and the first two weeks of October, 2008. The excavation was jointly directed by Mark Graham of Grampus Heritage Ltd., and Jan Walker, archaeological contractor. Faye McNamara of Tullie House Museum also supervised. A 25m x 2m trench north-west by south-east was opened and subsequently extended 6m x 2m on the west side. Several phases of walling were exposed, interpreted as the south wall of the cloister, the refectory building and the warming room, with an associated midden and extensive robber pits and trenches and discarded architectural fragments. Two graves were also located with an associated grave slab. A quantity of pottery, well preserved animal bone, remains of shell fish, lead, three coins and a copper alloy weight were also recovered.

The turf was manually removed, then the topsoil (101). Immediately below the topsoil was a layer of fragmented red sandstone (101, 102, 104). This had presumably been exposed and had weathered – there was no indication or record that the field has ever been ploughed. It produced pottery dating to the 19th and 20th century. This overlaid a mass of worked red sandstone architectural fragments. Initially it was thought these had been dumped as unusable building material, as at Bordesley Abbey (Greene, 1992, p. 196) but it seems likely that some of the remains at least fell from the east range and are *in situ* where they fell, as it proved possible at a later date using the plan to reconstruct at least one arch. This fall of the east range dates from the 17th–18th century according to stratified pottery (*113*, Fig. 11).

The architectural fragments in the central part of the trench were excavated and recorded and then removed. At this point the extension was dug, 6m x 2m to the west of the centre of the trench, to expose a wall and pillar showing in the south western section. Beneath the architectural fragments there was a thin burnt layer of sandy black loam, approximately 50mm thick, which spread over the whole of the north and centre of the trench, though not the extension (129, 153, 154). The pottery is indeterminate and could be 17th or 18th century. A series of robber trenches and pits testified to the removal of stone; Pit 165 at the north west corner, dating to post 17th–18th century, robber trenches (151) and robbed out drain (*150/159*). In the centre of the trench, and robber trench (152) cutting (151) and overlying the foundations of the south wall of the cloister (*176*, Fig. 12) date to post 16th–17th century. A layer of destruction debris (140) which included the weight is post 16th–17th century. The burnt layer overlay flags of red sandstone (*134*) and a clay floor (*135*) in the central area of the trench and a hearth (178) associated with a length of walling which was indicative of a chimney (*114*, Fig. 12, Pl. 4).

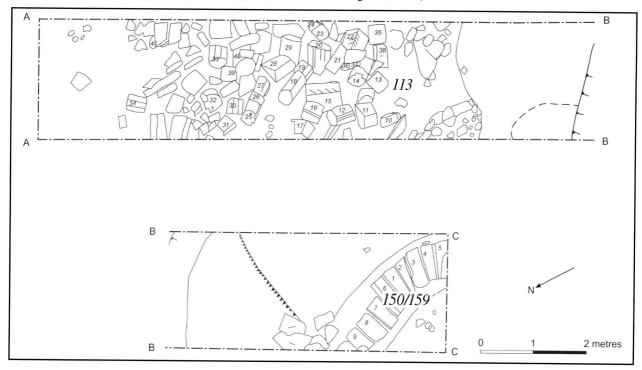

Figure 11: Plan of the 2008 trench showing architectural fragments (113)

Plate 4: 2008 trench, looking south west; view of the fireplace (178)

The facing stones had been robbed in the 17th or 18th century on pottery evidence leaving a wall core of thin red sandstone slabs. Further excavation in the extended area revealed a wall running north west–south east with a pillar in the corner (*138, 139*, Fig. 12, Pl. 5).

Overlying debris and tumble from the wall (146) dates to the 16th century at the earliest. Substantial granite boulder foundation stones (*141*) were found in the south end of the trench continuous with the wall and underlying it. A substantial midden dating to the 16th–mid-17th century overlaid these foundations.

Plate 5: 2008 trench, looking west; view of pillar base

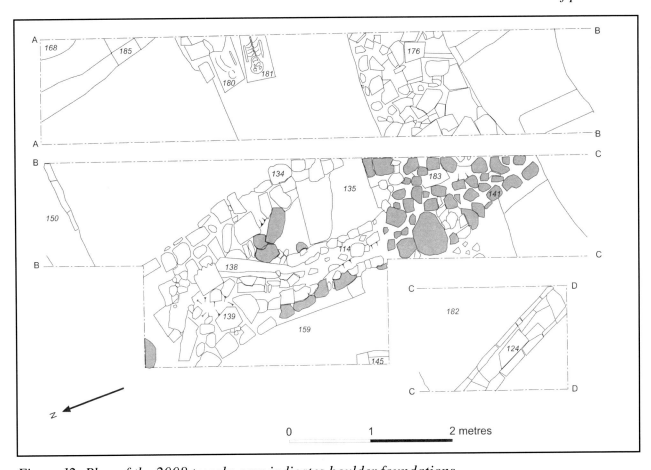

Figure 12: Plan of the 2008 trench: grey indicates boulder foundations

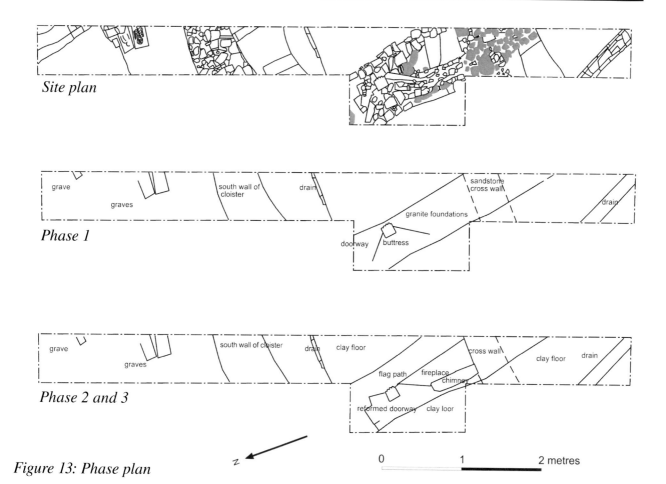

Site plan

Phase 1

Phase 2 and 3

Figure 13: Phase plan

0   1   2 metres

Phase 1

A wall ran north west–south east with another one at right angles to it at the south end of the trench, butting onto it and running north east– south west (*183*, Figs. 12 and 13). A possible triangular tower was at the north end of this wall in the extension area, with a doorway to the north of it.

Phase 2

The doorway was modified and buttressed.

Phase 3

The fireplace was added and the chimney built.

Flag floor remnants on a clay floor foundation in the extension to the west of the wall indicate that the wall sub-divides 2 rooms.

The north east–south west wall had been robbed out, removing the corner of the fireplace.

Two drains were found, one running north west –south east at the south end of the trench, and the other running east–west across the centre of the trench (*150/159*). The first drain, (*124*, Fig. 12) was filled in the 16th–mid-17th century. Drain *150/159* had been robbed out and all the stone removed except for a few slabs on the south side. The robbing took place post 16th–mid-17th century on pottery evidence and stratigraphically the drain is medieval.

To the north of the south cloister wall below the burnt area two skeletons were found (*180, 181,* Fig. 12, Pl. 6) partially under the eastern baulk. These were sealed by burning and debris. On stratigraphic evidence they date before the 16th– mid-17th century. They were excavated to a depth of 5-8cms. The cut width of *180* was 48cms and of *181* was 58cms. The skeletons were recorded and left *in situ*.

23

A grave slab was associated with grave 181 which was exposed fully when backfilling (Fig. 12). Both skeletons were male with teeth in good condition. No grave goods were found. Immediately overlying the graves was a scatter of coffin nails but no trace of the coffin timber survived.

A further grave slab was partially visible in the Eastern section (*185*, Fig. 12). The skeleton had been removed by later stone robbing but the cut of the grave was recorded as 45cms wide and 5cms deep. A further possible grave was located at the north end of the trench but was not investigated; heavy rain caused this end of the trench to flood.

Interpretation

The east to west wall foundations (*176*, Fig. 12) are very probably the south wall of the cloister. The monks are likely to have used Pythagoras' Theorem (Stalley, 1999) to lay out the cloisters; in a blind experiment we replicated this measurement from the surviving nave of the Abbey at the point where the cloister can be seen at right angles to the proposed extent of the southern aisle and the tape fell exactly along the line of the east–west wall. This would mean that the burials are located along the east wall of the cloister, which would lie just to the east of the trench.

The building uncovered to the south of the cloister (*114, 138, 139, 183*, Fig. 12) is likely to represent the remains of the east wall of the refectory, with a warming room to the east accounting for the fireplace and chimney. Comparative plans at other Cistercian foundations at Dundrennan Abbey, Dumfries and Galloway, and Roche Abbey, Yorkshire, show a similar layout. The drain running across the south end of the trench is also consistent with this theory and its line meets the drain discovered in the 2010 excavation season.

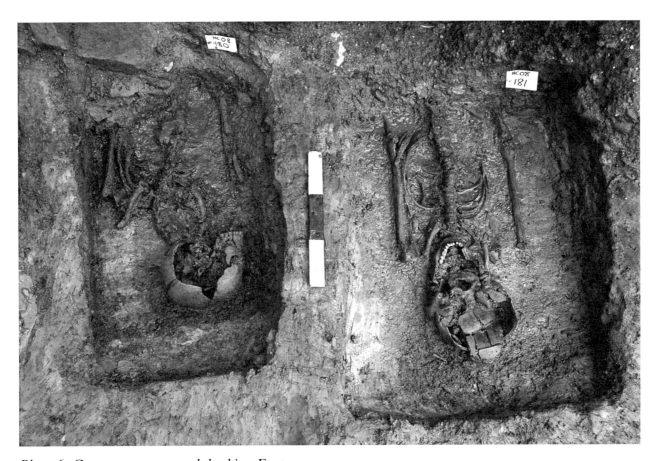

Plate 6: Graves as excavated, looking East

THE 2009 EXCAVATION

The area for the 2009 excavation was selected as a result of the 2008 excavations, guided by interpretation of the magnetometry survey. It was positioned to locate the south west corner of the cloisters and to investigate strong magnetic anomalies on the supposed eastern side of the cloisters and to the south of the south west corner. A trench 15m north–south and 4m east–west was opened by hand.

The topsoil was removed and the remains of a 19th century animal shelter found at the south end of the trench. Much of the south end was heavily disturbed by a deep pit producing 19th century pottery at the earliest. This was overlaid by a small four post structure, possibly an animal shelter, dating to the 19th–20th century. Below the topsoil was a layer of fragmented red sandstone in sandy brown loam (1001, *1004*, Fig. 14). Pottery from this dated at the latest to the mid-17th–18th century. When this was removed a layer of crushed red sandstone (*1012*) was exposed at the north end of the trench, sloping to the east and west. This was interpreted as the foundations of the cloister walk and produced only medieval pottery. A very small

(50cm diam.) patch of pebbles set in red clay overlay this, possibly the remains of a pebbled surface to the cloister walk. A shallow slot packed with clay running north – south down the centre of this may represent a drain (1014, 1015 and 1017, Fig. 14). The slot dates stratigraphically to the 13th–mid-17th century. To the west of this was a robbed out trench (*1013*, Fig. 14) running north–south along the west edge of the trench. This was interpreted as the foundation trench for the west wall of the cloister. The cut dated stratigraphically to the 13th – mid-17th century. The fill was brown sandy loam with fragments of red sandstone and mortar. Secondary robbing had taken place at the northern end (1009). The foundation trench (*1013*, Fig. 14) extended the whole length of the excavation, beyond the limit of the cloister, indicating it may also be the eastern extent of a western range of buildings. The robbing is post mid-17th century and pre 19th century in date.

A short section of extant medieval stonework was observed and recorded in the northern boundary wall of the field to the south of the church. This is interpreted as the northern junction of the western cloister wall, adjoining a surviving remnant of the original wall of the south aisle of the Abbey church (Pl. 7).

Plate 7: Northern junction of western cloister wall

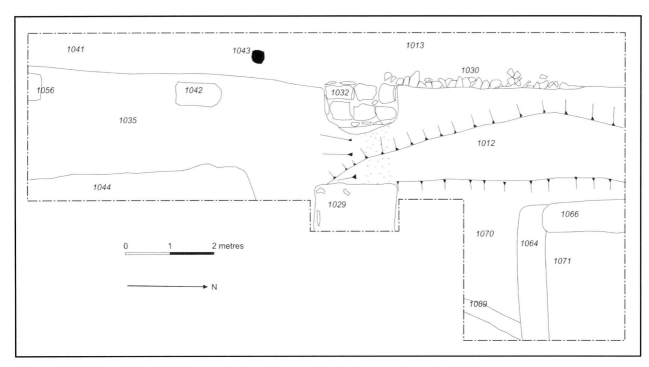

Figure 14: Plan of the 2009 trench, showing south cloister wall and robbing

Cobbles (*1030*, Fig. 14, Pl. 8) were set in the orange clay lining the eastern side of the foundation trench. These were laid later than the south wall of the cloister (*1032*, Fig. 14, Pl. 8) which was represented by a short length of foundation stones consisting of red sandstone slabs running east–west. These slabs form the base of the western side of an entrance into the cloister from the south and were presumably missed by the stone robbers following the line of the north–south wall.

An extension was dug on the east side of the trench, 2·3m north–south and 1m east–west which demonstrated the south walls of the cloisters continued (Fig. 15) after a gap in the centre of the trench which was interpreted as a doorway. A dark rectangular patch of burnt loam with charcoal inclusions and clay running east–west across the doorway may be a threshold.

Plate 8: 2009 Trench looking North East, showing foundations of south cloister wall and later cobbles in robbed out foundations of western cloister wall

Plate 9: Foundations of south cloister wall, looking east and construction ramp layer 1035

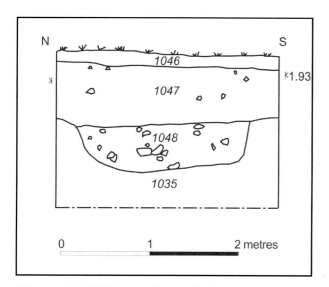

Figure 15: 2009 trench, south cloister wall, eastern section

To demonstrate conclusively that the south west corner of the cloister had been found, after discussion with English Heritage inspector Andrew Davison, a machine was brought in and extended the north east corner of the trench 3·6m east–west and 3·8m north–south. This exposed the robbed out inner walls of the cloister as expected; the north to south wall (*1066*, Fig. 14, Pl. 10) cutting the east-west wall (*1064*, Fig. 14, Pl. 10). The fill of both robbed out foundation trenches was a mortary mix of dark brown loam with fragments of red sandstone. The wall trench (*1064*, Fig. 14) produced a token from the fill (1063, Fig. 14) which probably comes from Selkirk and dates to the time of the Dissolution (see coin and tokens report and Pl. 22 and 23). Pottery was consistent with this date; ranging from 16th to mid-17th century at the latest.

Plate 10: 2009 Trench: robbed out foundations of inner cloister walls, looking east

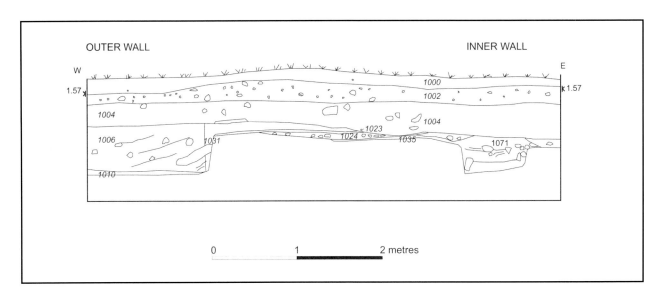

Figure 16: 2009 trench, northern section, showing cloister wall foundations

28

Robbed out trenches indicated two further walls running north–south on the east and west sides of the trench, outside and to the south of the cloisters (*1041, 1044,* Fig. 17). The foundation trench on the eastern side of the excavation contained tightly packed clay which appeared to bear the impression of planks running north–south. The entrance to the cloister from the south was ramped up with a construction layer of red brown gritty, clayey loam between the buildings outside the cloister (*1035,* Fig. 14, Pl. 9). This slumped into the foundation trench for the south wall of the cloister, and is therefore of a later date. A post pit (*1042,* Fig. 17) cutting this construction layer may be associated with the building of these walls. A second post pit similar in nature was found at the far south end of the trench (*1056,* Fig. 17) and possibly indicates these construction pits were associated with the building of the north to south wall (*1041,* Fig. 17) on the west side of the trench outside the cloister.

The construction layer was removed and beneath it an area of grey clay (*1038,* Fig. 17) was exposed, overlying natural subsoil. A possible timber slot was excavated (*1072,* Fig. 17) with several seemingly random post holes and pits. Some plough marks or alternatively drag marks from moving heavy stones were recorded and sampled but analysis was inconclusive.

Interpretation

The south west corner of the outer and inner cloisters was satisfactorily identified. All stone except for a few slabs has been robbed out probably by the local villagers looking for building material. An entrance to the cloisters from the south has been identified, and post holes and timber slots which predate the construction of the Abbey. Stratigraphically we can say that the south wall of the cloister was built first, then the north south wall on the western side of the trench. A ramp was constructed leading into the cloisters, and post pits dug into this may be associated with the north south wall on the western side, either as part of the construction phase for scaffolding or as piers to the east of the wall.

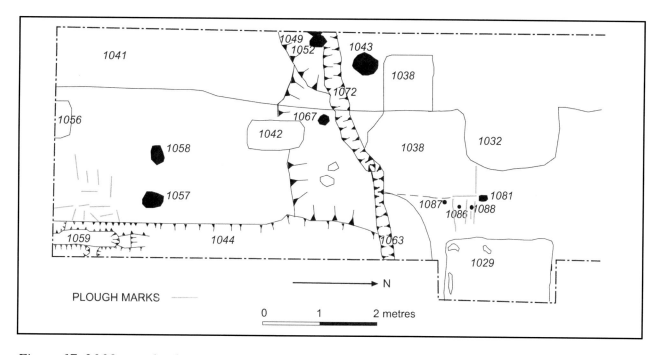

Figure 17: 2009 trench, showing possible early timber features

The 2009 evaluation trench

In the third week of November 2009 WCAS opened up the evaluation trench ET2 10m x 1m running north–south to the west of the stony hedge line field boundary i.e. to the north–east of the eastern side of the cloisters. It was to investigate the supposed position of the chapter house as discovered in 1906 (Baxter, 1907, 126-130). The turf and topsoil were removed manually. Beneath the topsoil was a layer of gritty brown loam with red sandstone and mortar inclusions which sealed the remains of a wall. There was much root disturbance from the hedge. The wall was robbed of its facing stones, and consisted of red sandstone and mortar. It ran east–west across the southern end of the trench. In the centre of the trench a tumble of red sandstone, mortar and architectural fragments, likely to have come from a ribbed vault of high status, were found (Fig. 27). To the north end there was a probable robber trench running east west, consisting of red sandstone fragments.

Plate 11: 2009 evaluation trench, showing possible north and south walls of chapter house looking south

Plate 12: November 2009, looking south from the chapter house; flooding in surrounding fields

Between the walls there was another layer of sandstone debris below which was evidence of burning.

It was not possible to complete the excavation as on the Thursday (19th November) Cumbria was hit by extensive flooding. The co-director, Mark Graham, was confined to Cockermouth, and Holme Cultram was virtually cut off, so, although the trench remained dry and workable, no one could reach it.

The floods did, however, illustrate the topography of Holme Cultram as it was surrounded by water from the overflowing river, and the scene is likely to reflect the marshy wet conditions around the Abbey when it was built in the 12th century (Pl. 12). It was concluded that the remains of the north and south wall foundations of the chapter house had been found, with possibly a central arch.

The 2010 evaluation trench

In February 2010 the evaluation trench ET1 10m north–south x 1m east–west was opened to investigate an anomaly in the cloister area, showing on the 2006 geophysics result. The anomaly appeared to be rectangular and also appeared on aerial photographs – indeed it is visible on the ground. Optimistically it was thought that it might represent an early church, such as that found by geophysics in the cloister area of Rievaulx Abbey, Yorkshire (Coppack, 1998, 36). In fact little was found to explain it; there was no evidence of banks or the remains of walls below ground level in section or in plan. A cobble surface was found and the remnants of two possible post pads which predated the cobbled surface. These may represent early timber buildings on the site when the monks first arrived.

The anomaly may possibly be a track way to the graveyard.

Plate 13: 2010 evaluation trench; post pad

The 2010 excavation

In 2010 it was decided to investigate the southern end of the eastern range. We re-examined the 1976 resistivity plot, and targeted several dark anomalies in the south–eastern corner of the field, in the hope of finding the latrines or, at least, the main drain. We also hoped to tie in any buildings with the 2008 excavations.

A trench 20m east-west and 3m north-south was opened up by hand and the turf and topsoil removed. Immediately beneath the topsoil at the west end of the trench were the remains of two parallel walls, running north–south. These walls proved very insubstantial on excavation. The west wall was probably a field boundary. The east wall showed some evidence of the base of a cruck and dated stratigraphically to the 17th–18th century, but no further evidence of a further wall to the west survived. The walls

were removed and more substantial remains were uncovered consisting of a wall running east–west in the western corner of the site, on a cobble foundation (22, 23, Fig. 18). This had been buttressed at a later date.

The site had been heavily robbed of stone. However there appeared to be the remains of a flagged area, largely robbed out, to the south and east of the wall and buttress (46, Fig. 18, Pl. 14). A curved line of stones indicated a possible drainage channel, (54, Fig. 18) draining into a feature on the southern edge of the trench which was probably a drain running north–south, though it was too near the baulk to determine this with certainty (53, Fig. 18).

A second line of stones was uncovered to the east of the flagged area aligned east–west, on the north side of the trench (59, Fig. 18). This is probably the foundations for a later wall; the

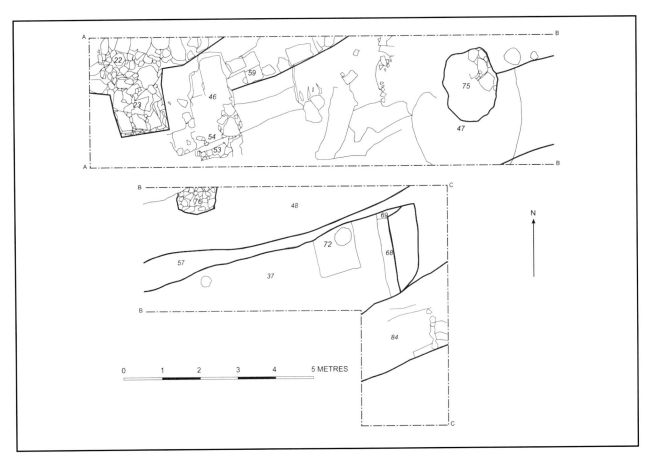

Figure 18: plan of 2010 trench

stones were cut and some faced on the south side and they were bonded together with clay. Some of the stones had been robbed out and pick marks indicated their original position. The foundations are quite different from the cobbled foundations of the wall and buttress.

Various channels had been dug in the area, probably representing drainage management.

Plate 14: 2010 trench, looking east

The eastern end of the trench was covered with a large amount of demolition material. The rubble layer produced a number of floor tiles – all different. The decision was made after consultation with English Heritage to remove the demolition material by machine. The demolition layer sealed a large pit cutting a gulley (37, Fig. 18), the latter being filled with demolition material. The gulley was 18cm deep and 2·1m wide. This material dated to the late 17th–18th century. A post hole to the south of the gulley cut the feature (72, Fig. 18); there were also postholes along both edges of the gulley.

These were earlier than 17th–18th century in date. The south side of the gulley was silted up, indicating water flow. A drainage channel (68, Fig. 15) led from the gulley to a deep feature at the edge of the excavation. Three foundation trenches formed an open square at the east end of the trench; the fill of these dated to the 17th–18th century. The decision was made to extend the trench which was done in late June, using a machine, to ascertain the nature of this feature, which turned out to be a substantial drain (84, Fig. 18). The upper layer of the drain was filled with demolition material, indicating robbing in the 17th–18th century, but at the bottom dressed stones were encountered. The drain was probably originally stone lined and then robbed. The lowest layer consisted of organic material including some wood samples.

Predating the gulley and dug into the natural clay were two large pits filled with river worn cobbles and packed with redeposited natural clay (75, 76, Fig. 18, Pl. 15). They formed substantial foundations and were interpreted as the bases for the arch of an undercroft at the south end of the east range. Similar pits were looked for at appropriate intervals to the south and west but none were found.

Plate 15: 2010 trench; pit 75

Interpretation

The cobble foundations and wall and buttress at the west end of the trench appear to line up with the walls of the 2008 excavations, and provisionally represent the rear south wall of the refectory. The arch identified at the east end of the trench is probably the south end of the east range. The drain is seen as the main drain to the latrines which were normally sited at the south end of the east range. The gulley is problematic; the best interpretation is that it is probably to do with water management. It is later than the archway and it may be that the east range was rebuilt after Scottish raids, on a more modest scale, and the prime purpose of the area to the south was water management.

Cleaning of 1906 trenches, 2009

A couple of weekends in January 2009 were spent by WCAS clearing out the 1906 trench in the churchyard. The trench is still open, but was very badly overgrown with brambles and raspberry canes and hawthorn. WCAS members cleared the undergrowth and exposed part of the tile floor and doorway (Pl. 16) to establish its condition. It was also measured in accurately with a total station. The tiles were all terracotta, and there was some damage by roots and frost. The base of the trench was cleaned up and recorded and then the tiles were covered with 10cms of sand and permeable weed suppressing sheeting, before being backfilled further with soil against frost damage.

Plate 16: 1906 trench, looking north west

Plate 17: 1906 trench; detail of pillar base in doorway, north east side

Cleaning and re-excavation of 1906 trench, 2010

This took place over three days in October, 2010. The trench opened in 1906 on the bank forming the south side of the graveyard was examined on the graveyard side only as this area was unscheduled. The fence marked the boundary of the scheduled area into which the excavation did not venture, making for narrow working conditions. Stones were built up as a three course high revetment for the bank along the fence line.

The bank behind the fence line was dug out by hand; the fill was loose sandy brown soil with fragments of red sandstone and pebbles, producing artefacts dating entirely to the 20th century (bottles, china and wire frames for a graveyard cross and heart), confirming it was the fill of Hodgson's trench (Hodgson, 1907, 262-268). Along the hedge line, at the west end of the trench and running north–south, there was a layer of fine rubble and mortar over red sandstone foundations forming the core of a wall. At foundation level the area was undisturbed and medieval tiles were found. It seems likely that earlier measurements were taken from above, aligning on the rubble core of the wall and producing some inaccuracies.

The east wall of the south transept was located, with a doorway backfilled with 20th century fill, which extended over the east wall. The doorway had a possible staircase which would lead up to the dorter. The stone at the base of the trench was mortared and formed a flagged surface which was interpreted as a floor level. The east wall appeared to continue under the floor and stairs, and was therefore built first then the staircase added (Fig. 19, Pl. 18).

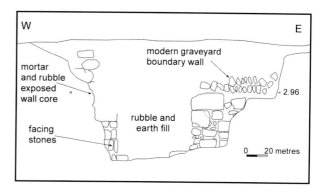

Figure 19: section drawing of 1906 trench

Plate 18: 1906 trench re-excavated; looking west and showing base of stairs

THE FINDS

Introduction

The most remarkable single find at Holme Cultram is probable the copper alloy weight. This may be a salt weight; Holme Cultram Abbey was renowned for export of salt and the 425gm weight (just under 1lb) would be appropriate for this purpose.

The environmental, glass and pottery reports and to some extent the floor tile report raise the question of spatial distribution. The horizontal distribution is as important as the vertical in the context of the excavation of abbey buildings. It seems likely that the Abbey was systematically dismantled and the glass removed to the area of the 2010 excavation where the lead cames were collected and glass discarded. The pottery cisterns all came from the region identified as near the kitchens and lay brothers' lodgings and were probably used for serving small ale. The functional nature of the pottery is also worth emphasising. In the environmental report it may in the future be possible to glean more from the spatial distribution of seeds and bones in different areas of the monastery, and identify diets consumed by different groups.

The Weight
Note from Alison Goodall

The coat of arms appears to be the royal arms; quarterly France (azure, fleur-de-lys or) and England (gules, three lions passant guardant or). The date depends on how many fleur-de-lys are shown in each quarter – as there are more than three the arms show 'France ancient' and the weight should date to between 1340 (when Edward III first quartered the arms of England and France) and c. 1400 (when the number of fleur-de-lys on the French arms was reduced to three).

The weight is made of copper alloy; they are more often made of lead or lead alloy. It is a well-made example. Examples are illustrated in G.Egan (1988, 311-317), where they were found in contexts from 1350-1450. Other undated examples are in D.Algar and G.Egan (2001, 126-7, Fig. 44-47). The Holme Cultram weight is larger than most, though no. 46 in the Salisbury Catalogue is a similar size and weight. Both approximate to 1lb. (454gms). The Holme Cultram weight weighs 425gms (15 oz).

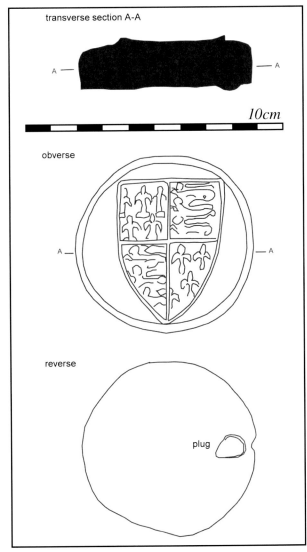

Figure 20: the weight; possibly used for weighing salt

The Grave Slab
Note from Lawrence Butler, Oxford University to Peter Ryder

The rustic cross would suggest a date of around 1350 though this style continues throughout the 15th century in the East Midlands. The initial cross is symmetrical with triangular serifs on all four terminals. The use of French and the cursive Lombardic script also suggest 1350 or earlier. However, the use of a book usually suggests a cleric or clerk; there is not really enough room for a chalice underneath it. The inscription reads

+ Ithone:denketvncgk:ici gist [desous] [Dieu:d]
e saalme:ey[:]Mercio[:a]me[n]+

The first letter is clearly an I so must be a version of Johannes. The second word is more problematic. The first three letters are DEN, and the next a rather angular K. The next is obliterated by a fracture in the stone but probably E T. The final group of letters are 'VNCGK 'or VNCGIC' This makes the reading 'DENKETNCGK' – probably DENKETUNOCK would be more plausible as a place name. The third word after the colon is clearly ICI, with the lower stop of the colon after it.

GIST is far from clear; only the G and the bottom serif of the I survive.

Along the left hand margin the general sense of the inscription is clear though some details are missing. The first word DIEU has gone. The second is DE. The third and fourth words are run together. It should read: SA: ALME. The words are ligatured at the top but there are hints of a cross bar on each A, showing as a small triangle on each left hand leg.

After the colon the fifth word should be EYT. Only the E is clear but there is room for one or two more letters (EY or EIT) and a colon.

Figure 21: the grave slab

There is a mark which could be the upper left arm of a Y but it is far from convincing. The sixth word MERCI is almost clear. Half the M survives.

The seventh and final letter is almost clear – AMEN. The left hand leg of the A with a prominent serif foot shows up well, but the remainder of the letter is lost. The M and E are clear. The N has been lost through damage and the final cross is too faint to be absolutely convincing with only its centre being certain.

On the cross two of the buds appear to be thorns. The cross shaft stands on a horizontal base. The top of the cross shaft ends in a jagged or serrated top.

Report on the Architectural Stonework
by Richard Wilson,
Historic Buildings Consultant

Context numbers in italics and stone numbers on figures 22 to 28 in brackets

Introduction

The three phases of excavation did not reveal large quantities of worked stone. This is probably a reflection of the way in which the Abbey was robbed of materials following the Dissolution. The lack of good building stone on the Solway Plain, where clay structures predominated until the much later introduction of brick, would have encouraged the people of Abbeytown to make full use of such a valuable source when it became available. All readily usable masonry was removed from the site, even to the extent of stripping out the foundations to the bare earth.

Many of the carved stones, with their often awkward shapes, would have presented more of a problem, as they were usually unsuitable for general walling. Approximately rectangular blocks could be roughly adapted by hacking off the raised decoration, and it is likely that the fragments described here were leftovers from such operations. Larger pieces of tracery would be almost incapable of such treatment. This might explain why many still exist on the site, or have been re-erected as decorative features in local gardens.

Whilst the complete disappearance of so many structures is a hindrance in the task of determining the building history of Holme Cultram, the accidental survival of decorative stonework is a useful diagnostic aid.

The following notes describe a representative selection of worked stones found during the three excavations.

Thanks are due to Peter Ryder, historic buildings consultant, for his observations and advice.

2008 Excavation

Moulded Stone from Column
HC08 *113* (20, Fig. 22.1)
This large fragment of red sandstone is 305cm long, and retains both bedding joints and an incomplete moulded face. The profile matches the *in situ* column base (*138*), and the stone may either have originated from this, or from a corresponding pillar in the vicinity. The surfaces are eroded, which suggests prolonged exposure to the elements following demolition. Whilst it is difficult to place a date on specific mouldings, the absence of deep hollows between the rolls in this example (a later refinement) and the alignment of one of the fillets with the chamfer, point towards the early 13th century (Bloxam, 1843, 34).

Voussoir from Arch
HC08 *113* (Fig. 22.2)
The mouldings have mostly been lost from this piece of red sandstone, but it survives to its full length. Both the outer and inner curved faces are only roughly finished, as if not intended to be seen. From this it can be inferred that this stone formed part of a wider moulding, made up of lines of voussoirs place side by side, arranged concentrically around the arch of a large window or doorway. Surviving detail is limited to a chamfer and small roll moulding.

Voussoir from Ribbed Vault
HC08 *113* (14, Fig. 23.3)
One of eighteen similar stones found within a concentrated area of the excavation. All are red sandstone, with an identical profile but of varying lengths. Similar stones can be seen partly exposed at the north end of the Glebe Field, immediately to the south of the church. The form of the moulding was widespread throughout the

medieval period, and it is therefore impossible to be precise; Peter Ryder believes that the angle of the chamfers is indicative of a post-Norman date. The plain character of the ribs implies that they are likely to have been in use in the more utilitarian parts of the monastery, most probably in areas where security or risk of fire were considerations. Most of the stones appear to be straight, but the angles of the bedding joints dictate the radius of the curve when the stones are placed together (Pl. 19). A few appear to have been left as they fell during demolition (HC08 18, 19 and 25, 26 and 27). All the bed joints are marked with a prominent X on one side, as a guide for correct alignment during construction. Masons' marks are also discernible on some examples. The rear face of each stone is rebated to support the web of the vault.

Assuming the geometry of the arch was set out from the soffit of the voussoirs, the radius of the curve would have been close to 2·51m, or 8 feet 3 inches. If it was constructed as a two-centred equilateral arch, the span would have been the same, and would closely correspond to the spacing of the cobbled foundation pads exposed during the 2010 excavation (75, 76, Fig. 18). These conditions would be appropriate for a transverse rib – parallel with the sides of the room – whereas a diagonal rib would have required a greater span, with the curve tending to flatten towards the crown of the vault. The sides of HC18 and HC19 have been cut away to a shallow angle. It appears that they were located at the springing of the vault, at the point where the ribs diverge from above the column or angle between the walls.

Attempts to accurately reconstruct the vaults at Holme Cultram are complicated by the variety of ways in which these features could be built. Some, as at Fountains, did not incorporate ribs across the ridges, while at Lanercost, the vaults of the south cloister range were built to a shallow

segmental profile, rather than the usual pointed arch. Further excavation may reveal keystones, which would greatly advance the understanding of the construction.

Rhomboidal Blocks

HC08 *113* (21, Figs. 23.4a, 4b)

These are two examples of seven large blocks of red sandstone found mingled together with the ribs already described. Their purpose has so far eluded any convincing explanation. All original surfaces have been brought to a fine finish, and have not suffered significantly from erosion. The tooling closely resembles that of the dressed masonry exposed in the area of the south transept, a 1906 excavation reopened in 2010. The stones all share the same distinctive shape, but vary in length. Two faces of each stone, as originally cut, were rhomboidal in form, with parallel sides of two different lengths. Instead of coming to a sharp point, each of the acute angles terminated with a narrow fillet, one perpendicular to one of the sides, the other angled to two edges. Alongside the perpendicular fillet, on the flanking sides, was a deeply cut 'X'. It is safe to assume that, as in the case of the ribs, this mark was an instruction for the correct orientation of the stones during construction. Scored setting-out lines and masons' marks can be seen in places, among which is a distinctive interleaved 'W'. The blocks perfectly align when placed one on top of another on their rhomboidal faces. This ties in with the position of the 'X' marks, and suggests that the stones were laid in a horizontal line (such as a parapet) or vertically (as a column), rather than being used individually as, for instance, buttress offsets. The lack of wear leads to the conclusion that the blocks were not exposed to the weather long enough for erosion to become apparent (indicating a construction date shortly predating the demolition); alternatively they could have been internal elements, protected from the weather, and could therefore belong to a wider date range. Some of the stones have been crudely adapted at a later period to suit a different purpose. It is not clear if this work was carried out during the life of the monastery or afterwards, but the standard of the roughly cut faces and mortises contrasts dramatically with the original finishes.

String Course Type A

HC08 *113* (04, Fig. 24.5)

Three intact stones with a semi-octagonal nosing were reused as parts of a drain, laid during a later phase in the life of the claustral buildings. They clearly formed part of a string course, the simple profile and degree of erosion suggesting that they may date from the Transitional period, around the date of the church's construction. A similar string course is illustrated in Bloxam (1843, 87) and Atkinson (1946, Fig. 163).

String Course Type B

HC08 *113* (Fig. 24.6)

A single, full-length stone found in the same location as HC08 *113* (04), and adapted for the same purpose. The rounded profile comes to a point, similar to the 'keeled mouldings' which seem to have appeared during the transition from the Romanesque, and which remained popular throughout the 13th Century and beyond.

String Course Type C

HC08 *157* (Fig. 24.7)

This is a large fragment, featuring a prominent roll moulding, which is returned around one end. Similar mouldings were often incorporated in the plinths of large buildings, usually forming the top course (Roberts, 1977, 7, Fig. 2).

The generic profile was in use for much of the medieval period, and it is consequently difficult to place a date on it. The degree of erosion suggests that it might belong to one of the earlier phases.

Chimney Capstone

HC10   (Fig. 24.8)

The purpose of this stone was identified by Peter Ryder. The chimney was octagonal in plan, made up of four segments, of which this is one. Special treatment to this stone – the rounded top edge, and fine tooling to the upper part of the interior – implies that it formed part of the cap. Few rooms were equipped with fireplaces, and the context of this find leads to the conclusion that it may have come from the warming room.

String Course Fragment

HC08 *101* (Fig. 25.9)

This is representative of a number of small fragments of moulding found in the vicinity of the wall dividing the refectory from the warming room. In contrast to the string course components described above, the mouldings are much finer in detail and finish, implying that they formed part of the interior decoration. This particular stone was from the upper part of an internal string course, or possibly the abacus of a capital. Numerous examples of the pointed roll have been found at various locations around the site, which suggests that there was a major building phase in the 13th century, when this decorative element seems to have reached its height.

2009 Excavation

Fragment of Piscina

HC08 *107* (Fig. 25.10)

This finely moulded piece of red sandstone was identified as part of the bowl of a piscina by Peter Ryder. It was found in a midden dating to the 16th–mid-17th century. It was probably square in plan, one half of the bowl being sheltered under a carved niche in the thickness of the wall. The fragment belongs to that part of the bowl which was corbelled out from the wall face. The scalloped or fluted interior is a common characteristic. All surfaces except the bowl and its surround show signs of having been painted with white limewash. The moulding contains diminutive forms of elements seen on other finds, such as the alternating hollows and rounds, used in combination with fillets and chamfers. Without being too prescriptive, it would appear that this could also date to the 13th century.

Label Stop and Hood Mould Fragments
HC09 *1011, 1019* (Fig. 26.11, 12)
These are two pieces of carved red sandstone from the exterior of a window or doorway. As the section of both is identical, it is likely that they were located on the same building, possibly even on the same moulding. The profile is probably best described as a double filleted roll with a hollow soffit. One piece is curved along its length, and the soffit (which is on the inside of the curve), is less eroded in comparison with the other surfaces. This demonstrates the orientation of the moulding, and how it was designed to deflect rainwater from the top of the opening. The other piece formed the left hand termination of the hood mould, and was enriched with carved foliage. Although incomplete, enough remains of this carving to show how similar it was with a fragment of a capital found in 2010 (HC10 *08*). The double filleted roll and hollow soffit also appears at Rievaulx, as part of a much larger moulding (Paley, 1878, plate XVIII, Fig. 1), and is attributed to the Early English style – again within the supposed main building phase of the 13th century.

Fragment of Roll and Fillet Moulding
HC09 ET2 *016* (Fig. 26.13)
Many examples of this moulding were found, particularly in the excavations of 2009 and 2010; this piece of red sandstone is unusual, but not unique, in featuring a deep score along the centre of the fillet. It was also limewashed, the accumulated coats amounting to a thickness of 1mm. The function of the scored line is not clear. It is too fine and incorrectly positioned to have been intended as a rebate for glazing or

joinery, so it is conjectured that its purpose was to enliven the plain white decoration by casting a slight shadow across the face of the fillet. Alternatively, it could have formed an edge within a more elaborate scheme of polychromy, which was either never executed, or which was subsequently replaced with the surviving decoration.

Small Curved Moulding Fragment
HC09 *1008* (Fig. 26.14)
The small size of this piece of buff sandstone with its fragmentary moulding makes interpretation of its provenance difficult. Its fineness is consistent with items such as moulded capitals, or perhaps small basins. However, there is a slight indication that the carving was curved in two planes, which would invalidate these possibilities. Its main interest is in the unusual profile, which is concave on one side and convex on the other, and in the traces of limewash which remain in places.

Flat Moulding
HC09 *1011, 1019* (Fig. 27.15)
In two pieces, this incomplete moulding is symmetrical about the central fillet. The double roll on either side is flattened out, almost into the 'wave moulding' which is thought to have been used more widely in the Decorated period, following on from the middle of the 13th century (Morris, 1978, 21). The shallow depth in proportion to its width would make it a suitable motif for the vertical subdivision of panels in a large expanse of plain wall.

Fragment of Hood Moulding, String Course or Sill
HC09 *1010* (Fig. 27.16)
This weathered piece of red sandstone has a sloped upper surface to deflect water away from the face of the wall. The hollow below the fillet would probably have terminated with a smaller, raised fillet on the bottom edge of

the stone. According to Paley (1878, plate XVI and p56) and Atkinson (1946, Fig. 163), this type was most common in the Decorated and Perpendicular periods. It could conceivably have been used in conjunction with the flat moulding described above, as a horizontal division on a panelled wall.

Moulded Voussoirs

HC09 ET2 *010* (Figs. 27.17a; matching fragment were discovered in an exploratory trench on the presumed site of the chapter house. They are heavily moulded, made of red sandstone, and all the exposed surfaces have been painted with white limewash. The moulding is complex, and it incorporates a few supposedly Early English features, such as the roll and fillet (cf HC09 ET2 *016*) and bowtel, which are interspersed with deep hollows (Atkinson, 1946, 178). The rear faces of the stones are rebated in the same way as those of the plainer voussoirs discovered in 2008. This would suggest that they were also components of a ribbed vault, this time one of a higher status within the complex. Another possibility is that the rebates were to provide a key for adjoining stones to make up a larger moulding.

A projection of the curve produces a radius of approximately 1·77 metres (5'9 ¾"), which would be equal to the span if it was a two-centred equilateral arch.

2010 Excavation

Fragment of Carved Capital

HC10 *08* (Fig. 28.18)
This is an almost intact lobe from the capital of a small column. It is unusual in that it has been carved in a buff stone. The material may have been chosen for its workability; alternatively it could be an indication of a distinct building phase, when different sources of stone might have become available. The foliage is of the 'stiff-leaf' type, a characteristic motif of Early English stonecarving. The outer curve ends with a flattened return, which represents the meeting with the abacus, the horizontal moulding forming the top of the capital.

Interior String Course Fragments

HC10 *44* (Fig. 28.19)
The three fragments are parts of the same incomplete stone. The finely finished, unworn surface shows that it was located in a sheltered position. The pointed bowtel, already seen elsewhere on the site, has been scaled down to suit a small, carved feature, such as a niche or monument. The horizontal top surface has been lightly pecked to provide a key for bonding, and a scored line parallel with the edge probably represents the line of the masonry above.

Assorted Carved Stones recovered from the surface of the Glebe Field in 2010.

A preliminary examination has been made of a collection of worked stones which is mostly concentrated in the northwest corner of the field. Much remains to be done, but a few conclusions can already be drawn.

There are largely complete sections of tracery, mullions and jambs, among other items, and it should be possible to attempt a partial reconstruction of a window design from these, based on the combination of three components: the two surviving mullions, the larger quantity of 'V' shaped tracery, and, from the northeast corner of the field, a pair of larger 'X' shaped tracery stones. In plan, all share the same plain chamfered profile, in place of more elaborate mouldings. This variation is believed to have been in common use throughout the Early English and Decorated periods (Parker, 1994, 167).

The tracery was curvilinear, with repeated diamond shaped elements in alternating rows across the full height of the window head, referred to as reticulated work. Unfortunately, none of the voussoirs or sills have so far been discovered, so it is not yet possible to confirm how many windows were built to this design, nor how large they might have been.

Intact examples of reticulated windows are to be seen in the clerestory of the choir at Carlisle Cathedral (Pl. 20), which was rebuilt in this form in the second quarter of the 14th century (Alexander, 2004, 118), and the presence of a distinctive mason's mark at both sites encourages the belief that they might be contemporaneous. It is in the shape of a capital 'R', with elaborate serifs (Alexander, 2004, Fig. 21, 7rl), and at Holme Cultram can be found on the side of one of the two mullions (Pl. 21).

The remainder of the stones in the collection are mostly unconnected and have lost their original context, but they still hint at the former richness of the abbey buildings. They include what appear to be parts of a triple headed niche or arcade, a fragment of a castellated parapet, and numerous early period mouldings, some of which show evidence of adaptation in later building phases.

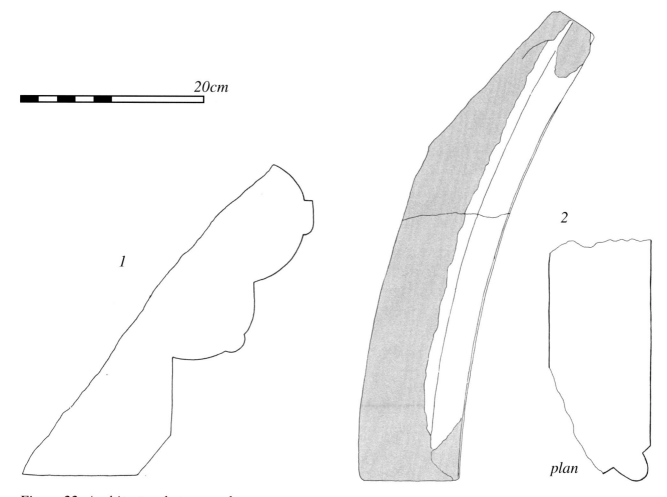

20cm

1

2

plan

Figure 22: Architectural stonework

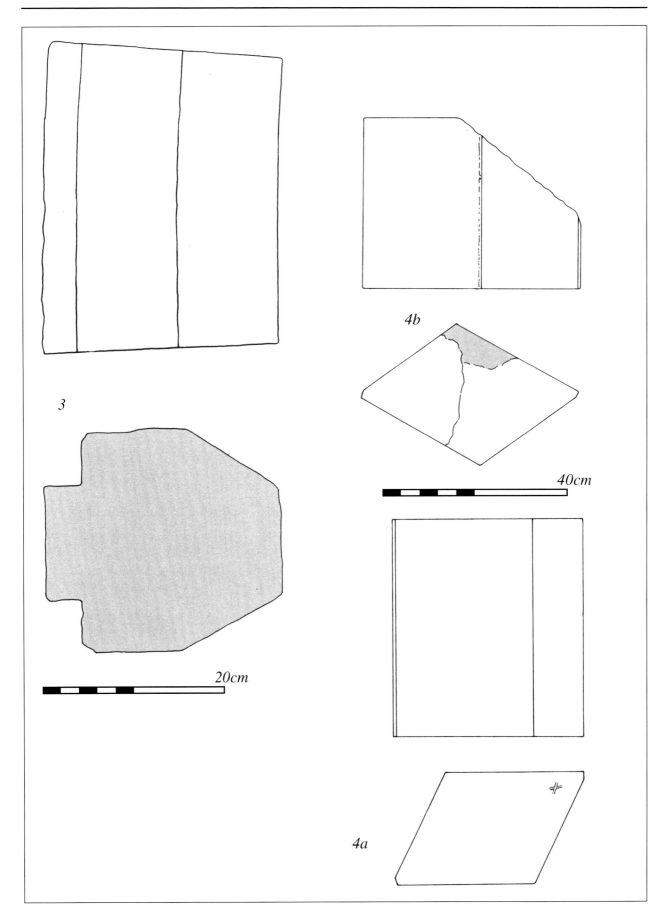

Figure 23: Architectural stonework

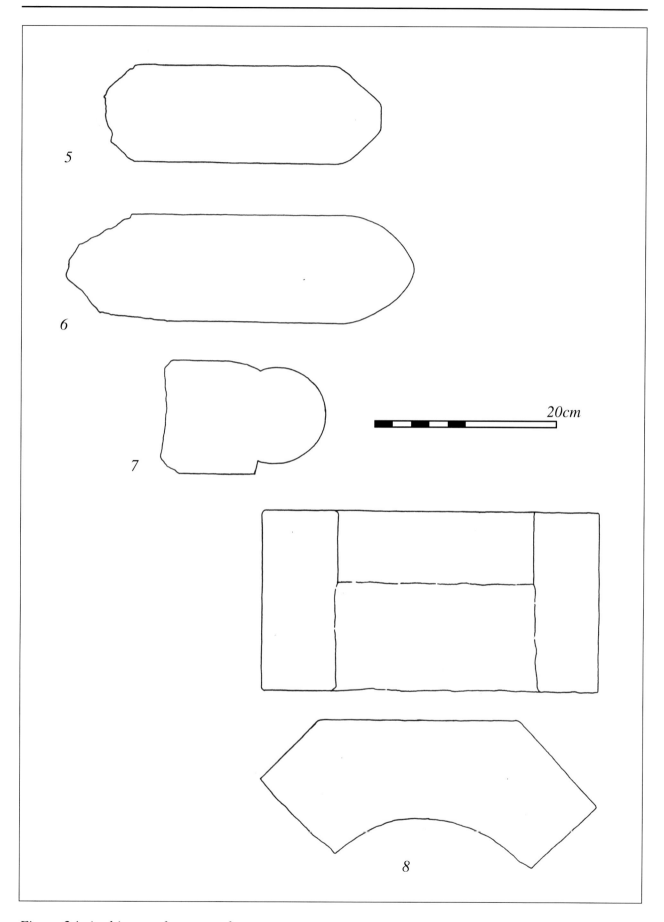

Figure 24: Architectural stonework

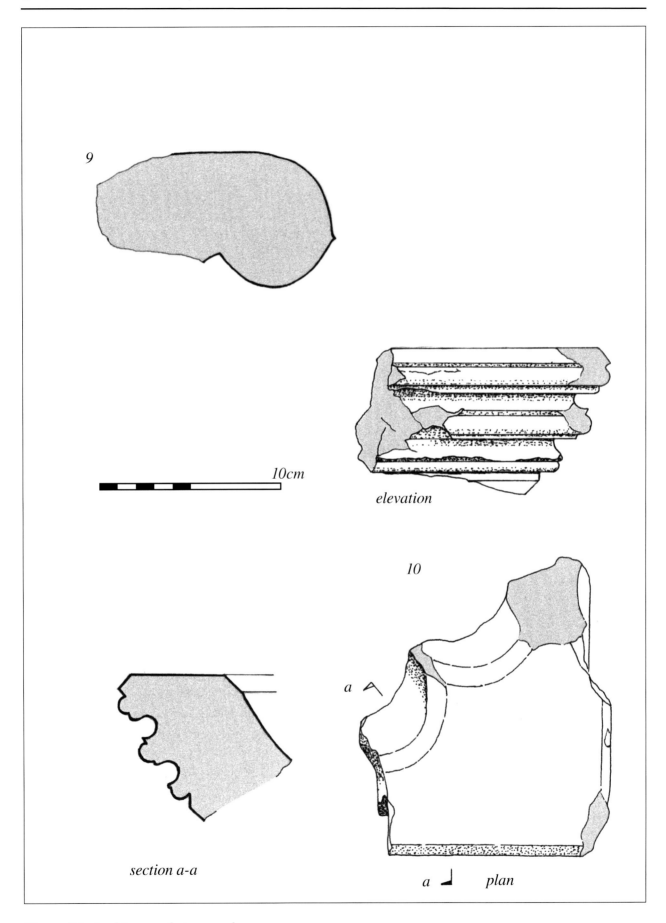

Figure 25: Architectural stonework

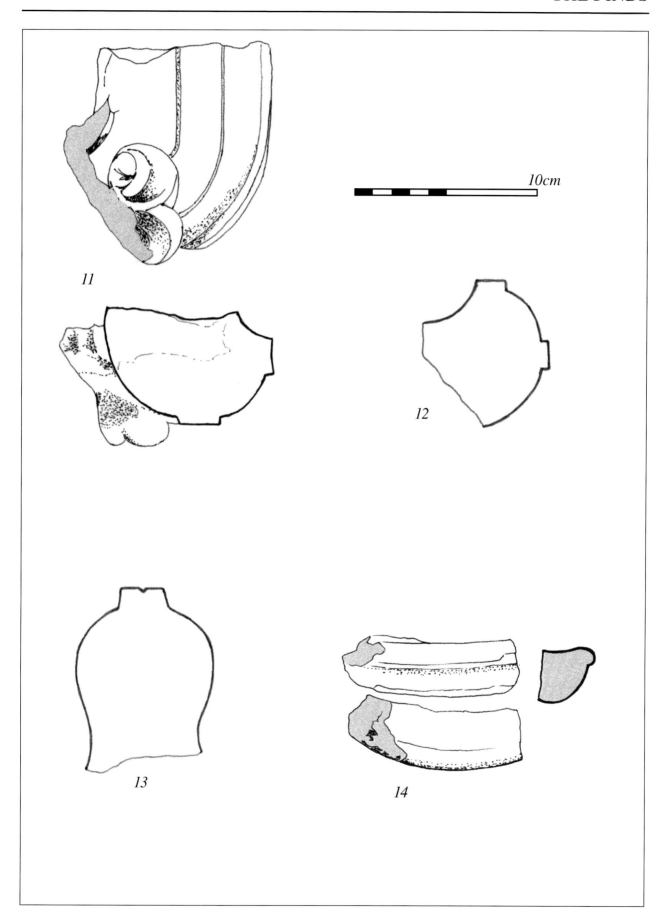

10cm

Figure 26: Architectural stonework

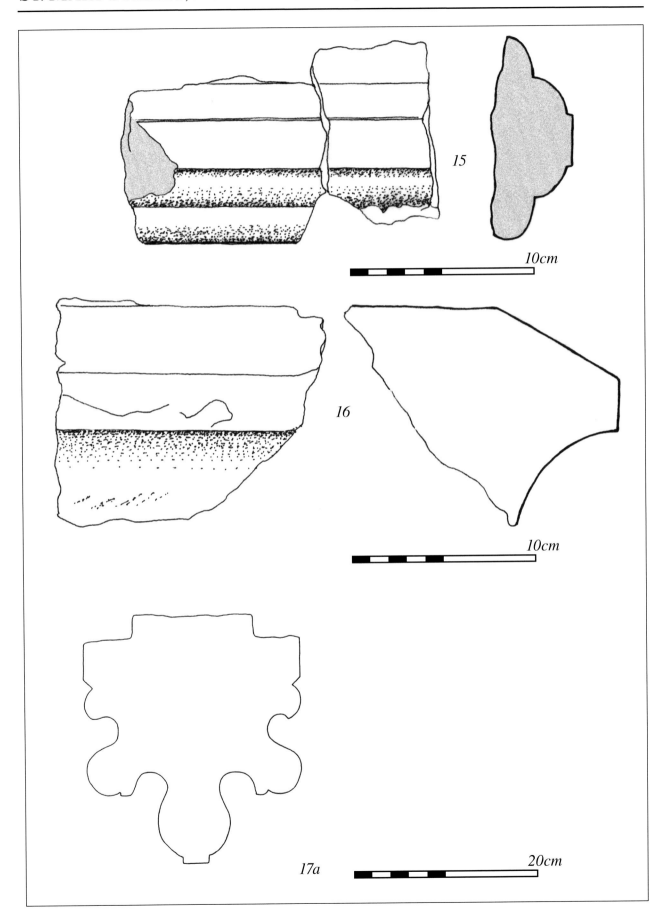

Figure 27: Architectural stonework

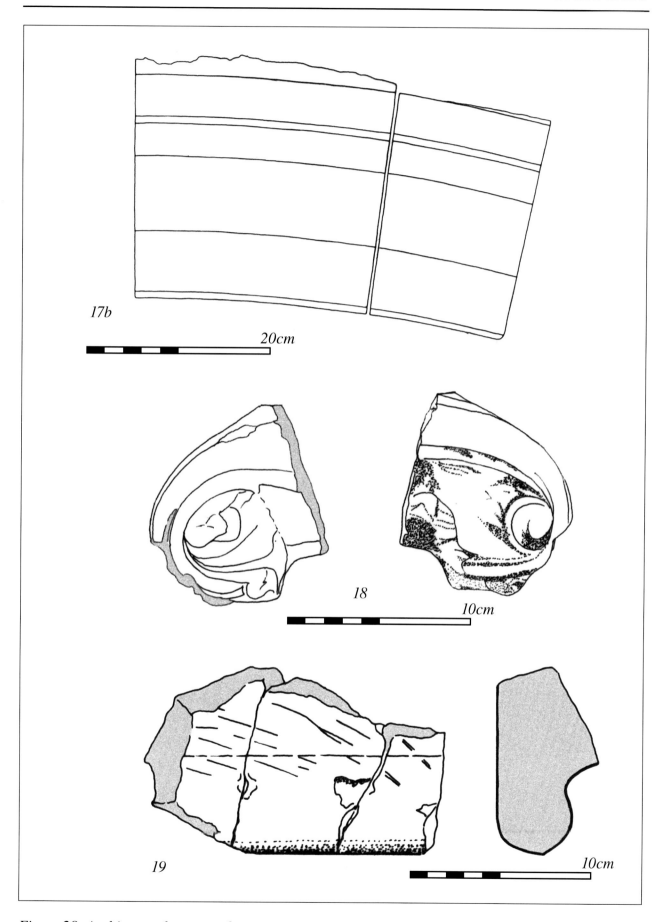

Figure 28: Architectural stonework

Plate 19: Reassembled vaulting rib

Plate 20: Carlisle Cathedral; window on clerestory of choir

Plate 21: Holme Cultram: mason's mark on mullion

Report on the Medieval floor tiles found at Holme Cultram Abbey excavations 2008 -2010

All references are to Stopford 2005

Summary

The present assemblage advances and refines the evidence for the use of medieval floor tiles at Holme Cultram Abbey. Drawings by Gilbanks (1899) and those of E and T H Hodgson (1907) provided much of what was previously known about the tiles from this site. These drawings were re-published, together with details of the then extant tiles, in a study of the production and use of floor tiles across northern England (Stopford, 2005, 189-91, Figs. 17.1-17.5; 250, Fig. 24.4; 302). The gazetteer entry for Holme Cultram in that study recorded that only 25 tiles were extant from the site, with many of these re-set in the church and not therefore fully visible. The material now recovered includes seven new designs and an extant example of one design previously only known from the antiquarian records. The new assemblage shows that example and six of the new designs, together with all the undecorated shaped tiles and 70mm squares, can be assigned to the Holme Cultram mosaic group (tile group 13 in Stopford, 2005, 190-1). These tiles provide important new detail of the manufacturing characteristics of this workshop. They enable clearer comparison with the Plain Mosaic tiled pavements used in the major monasteries of the north-east in the 13th century. They suggest that, while the Plain Mosaic pavements were the likely inspiration for Holme Cultram's mosaic paving, the tiles were not made by the same workshop.

The other new design is difficult to decipher and is represented only on two tiny triangles. These tiles and the line impressed design are part of a tile group known from both Holme Cultram and Carlisle Cathedral (Stopford, 2005, 250, tile group 28). They are thought, on typological grounds only, to be of later medieval date.

In addition, the Holme Cultram assemblage contains four fragments and one half tile of Plain-glazed type with nail-holes in at least some of the corners of their upper surfaces. Plain-glazed tiles were glazed either yellow/ brown or dark green with no decoration and were generally laid in a simple chequered arrangement of alternating light and dark tiles. Large numbers of Plain-glazed tiles, thought to have been imported from the Netherlands in the later 14th and 15th centuries, are found on sites in the UK. However, while the small and fragmentary nature of the extant examples from Holme Cultram makes interpretation difficult, they do not appear to be imports (in the terminology adopted in the 2005 study, they would be classed as Non-standard Plain-glazed; Stopford, 2005, chapters 5 and 20). A bigger sample might revise this view.

None of the tiles were found *in situ* or in contexts thought to indicate where they had once been laid at Holme Cultram.

The floor tiles

In the 2005 study, tiles from Holme Cultram were assigned to four groups (Stopford tile groups 12, 13, 14 and 28). These tile groups and their related design numbers are retained below, with revisions or additions as needed. The published characteristics of the groups are not repeated in full but any additional information from the new assemblage is set out in a similar format.

Tile Group 12 – antiquarian drawings
(Stopford 2005, 189-90 and Fig. 17.1)

Tile Group 12 consisted of four square tile designs known only from the antiquarian record from Holme Cultram (designs 12.1-12.4). The recently recovered assemblage contains one example of design 12.1. This shows that it was decorated using a technique known as 'reverse inlay' (in which the whole surface of a red tile body is coated with a layer of white clay, then lightly impressed with a design cut out on a wooden stamp and the indentations filled with a thin red clay slip). There are 11 other tiles decorated in reverse inlay in the assemblage. Two of these are of the hexagonal design 13.1, previously known only in counter-relief and assigned to Tile Group 13. The similarities between all these tiles strongly suggest that they, together with the extant undecorated mosaic shapes, were all the products of the same workshop. They are all therefore now assigned to Tile Group 13 and discussed below.

Tile Group 13 – Holme Cultram mosaic
(Stopford 2005, 190-2 and Fig. 17.2, 17.4-17.5)

Sample and condition:
68 tiles of which 11 are decorated, plus 6 unidentified fragments. The majority of the tiles are worn or broken although some decorated examples are in good condition. A broken tile (115mm across, probably square) of new design 12.8 is completely unworn but over fired and has part of another tile stuck to the glaze. This is likely to be a waster and may never have been laid in a floor. Four of the new designs are on small fragments.

Mosaic arrangements:
Mosaics M.36 (using the hexagonal tiles) and M.25 (a trellis arrangement) were identified in the antiquarian record. The extant even-sided hexagonal examples (S.58) and 10 examples of S.56 could be used in M.36. A single 53mm square could have been used in M.25 but no suitable rectangles are extant. Mosaic arrangement M.91 might be suggested by 12 examples of S.23 but there are several other possibilities for this shape (for example, Eames, 1980, II, IX, X or XXXV). An additional mosaic arrangement is suggested by one part tile, probably hexagonal but with two longer sides. Tiles of this shape could have been set around a central square as, for example, in Eames (1980, II, XLV).

Shapes, sizes:
Squares 53mm, *c*.70-75mm and *c*.115mm, S.23, S.56, S.58, S.60. It is notable that there were no shaped tiles with curved sides. The depth of the tiles varied between 35mm and 45mm.

Designs:
Design 13.1 on two even-sided hexagonal tiles; new design on a 70mm square (13.2); new design on a corner fragment, possibly a square (13.3); 1 part tile, probably hexagonal but with two longer sides, with new design (13.4); 1 part

square or rectangle 90mm across, new design (13.5); 1 part triangle with new design (13.5); 2 small fragments with new designs (12.6 and 12.7); a new design on *c*.115mm probably square tile (possible waster), (13.8); design on *c*.115mm square tile previously assigned to Tile Group 12, now 13.9 (Figs. 29 and 30).

Decoration:
All the newly discovered decorated tiles of Group 13 are decorated using the time consuming technique of reverse inlay. The layer of white clay on the decorated examples tends to be thick, up to 7mm, while the inlaid red clay is thin (less than 1mm), and probably applied as a slip. The tiles are glazed brown over the red clay and yellow over the white clay.

Nail holes:
None.

Firing:
Mainly oxidized apart from the over fired tile with design (13.8) which was largely reduced.

Fabric:
Sandy (*c*1mm) with occasional grog.

Treatment of tile sides:
None of the triangular tiles from Holme Cultram was scored and split as is usual in many medieval tile assemblages, nor were they cut, scored and split as was found among similar sized triangular tiles of the Plain Mosaic group (see Stopford, 2005, Fig. 10.22).

Treatment of bases:
There were no keys cut into the bases of the tiles.

Quality:
The tiles were competently made. The design stamps were comparatively poorly cut, the designs giving a slightly amateurish impression.

Discussion
The mosaic arrangements suggested by the tile shapes and the antiquarian record and the use of reverse inlay decoration are resonant of the Plain Mosaic tile workshop. Massive and elaborate Plain Mosaic pavements were installed in the churches of many Cistercian houses (but also elsewhere) in the north-east in the 13th century (Stopford, 2005, chapters 2 and 10). The mosaic tiles from Holme Cultram differ from those of the Plain Mosaic workshop in the absence of keys in the bases of the *c*.70mm square tiles, the way the triangles were cut out, the more completely oxidized fabrics and the relatively poorly cut design stamps. In addition, the two scroll designs (13.4 and 13.5) are unlike anything in the Plain Mosaic repertoire but are familiar from other tile groups.

It seems likely that the tiles at Holme Cultram were inspired by paving elsewhere, rather than being obtained from the same source. It may be notable that there are no shaped tiles with curved sides in the Holme Cultram assemblage and no evidence, therefore, for mosaic roundels or other more complex arrangements. These would have been more difficult to make and to lay in a pavement. Perhaps in a similar vein, all the extant decorated tiles are reverse inlaid so that the designs appear brown on a yellow background. In the Plain Mosaic series the relatively small numbers of these decorated tiles were made in two colour-ways, light on dark as well as dark on light. The interchange of these variations made the paving much more complex than the single colour-way apparently used at Holme Cultram. The assemblage seems likely to have been locally made.

Tile Group 14
(Stopford, 2005, 192 and Fig. 17. 5)

The assemblage provides no further evidence for line impressed mosaic at Holme Cultram as in Gilbanks' sketch of 1899.

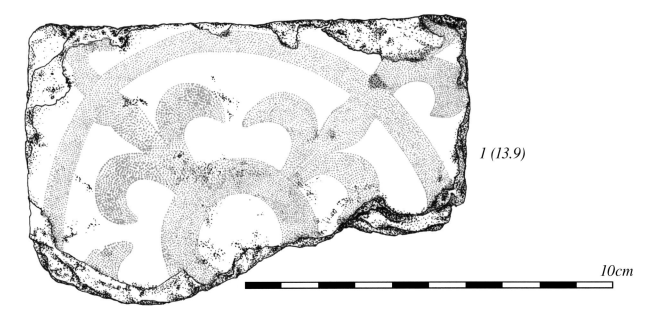

1 (13.9)

10cm

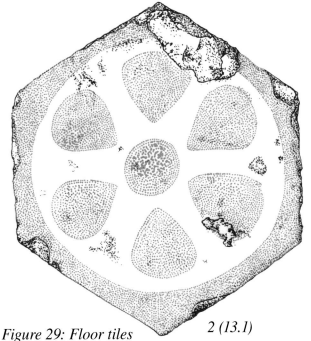

Figure 29: Floor tiles   *2 (13.1)*

Tile Group 28
(Stopford 2005, 250 and Fig. 24.4)

The assemblage contains one large fragment of a Group 28 tile with an almost black glaze over the line impressed design of 28.1. This example adds to the known tiles of this type from both Holme Cultram and Carlisle Cathedral. It is deeper than the other examples at 40mm, the base is uneven and sandied including quartz and grog of more than 3mm.

In addition there are two small triangular tiles of a new line impressed design (28.3) that very likely belongs to this tile group. This is suggested by the crudely cut line impressed design, the black glaze on one example and the depth of the tiles (40-45mm). The second triangle was glazed a dirty yellow over a poor quality slip. Although very likely to represent only part of a larger design, the triangular tiles were not scored and split from a larger tile but cut right through to the base.

A large and completely abraded fragment may also belong to this tile group.

Plain-glazed tiles
(Non-standard type)

Sample and condition:
Three fragments, one part triangle and one half square tile, all part worn.

Glaze:
Red brown and dark brown over partly reduced example, yellow brown over slip.

Shapes, sizes:
Square or triangular, 112mm across; tile depths 40-44mm.

Nail holes:
One found in the corner of all examples, *c.*20mm from the tile edges, possibly only in one corner of the half square.

Firing:
Oxidised extremities with a reduced core.

Fabric:
Fine sand. The clay was poorly mixed with cracking.

Treatment of tile sides:
Bevelled.

Treatment of bases:
Sandied, homogenous, no keys.

Quality:
Roughly made. The glaze on the broken edge of one tile shows that it cracked badly during firing. Another fragment had broken along a crack line that had formed in firing.

Discussion

The Plain-glazed sample is small but the tile characteristics suggest that they were not imports from the Netherlands. The depth of the tiles is greater than most imports, the part reduction in firing and the poorly prepared body fabric are not typical of Plain-glazed tiles from the Netherlands. Like the other tiles from this site they may have been locally made.

A single fragment, unglazed other than by drips from other tiles, with a nail-hole in the corner, could also be part of this group and be unglazed by accident. However this tile, at 30mm, is much thinner than the other examples and the fabric is poorly mixed including both white and red clay.

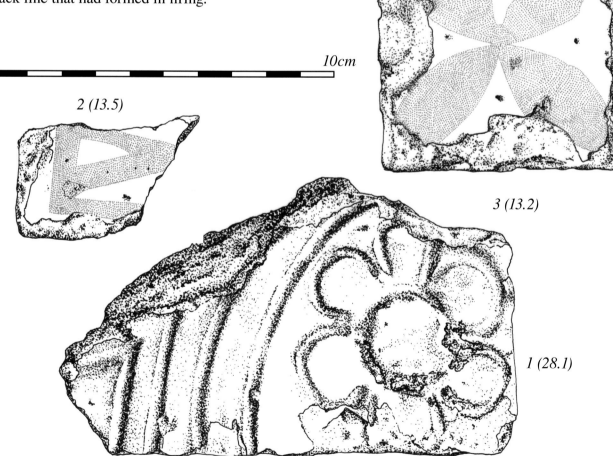

10cm

2 (13.5)

3 (13.2)

1 (28.1)

Figure 30: Floor tiles

Report on the window glass found at Holme Cultram Abbey excavations 2008 - 2010

Dr. Rachel Tyson

Numbers refer to archive catalogue

325 fragments of painted and 303 fragments of unpainted window glass were excavated from St. Mary's Abbey, Holme Cultram, between 2008 and 2010 by the West Cumbria Archaeology Society. The glass was examined to establish the date and glazing style of the windows. Other research aims were to examine whether the window glass was typical of that found in other Cistercian foundations, and whether it was possible to establish which buildings the glass came from.

The largest concentration of painted window glass was found in 2010, while far fewer fragments were found in the 2008 and 2009 excavations. The glass fragments were in a friable condition, either weathered opaque brown through the entire glass matrix or retaining a greenish-colourless glass core but with flaky opaque surfaces. The size of the majority of fragments was generally small (Fig. 32.40), although a rectangular quarry *c* 83mm x 53mm was unusually large compared to others. While a number of fragments had at least one grozed edge, there were few examples where the original glass quarry shape could be seen. It is likely that the windows were smashed before burial. Surviving grozed edges showed there were straight and curved edges, and acute, obtuse and right-angles between edges. Some small rectangular border quarries were evident. The paint was not always easily visible due to surface weathering and concretions from the surrounding soil. Where it was visible, it was red-brown, and painted in thick bold brush strokes. The later fragments had thinner, more cursive brush strokes. Some fragments had matt black paint with decoration 'picked out' with a hard thin implement (e.g. Fig. 35.174 and Fig. 36. 213). Shading and possible backpainting or silver stain is visible on a few fragments (e.g. (Fig. 35.179), but it may have disappeared on other fragments.

Where the original glass was still visible, it was pale greenish-colourless (known as 'white'); no coloured glass was identified, although it is possible that some fragments that are completely opaque now were originally coloured. The exceptions were four fragments which appeared very pale opaque blue or blue-green (Fig. 33.67, Fig. 34.72, 88, 89), but these were also very misshapen, probably heat-deformed, and the current colour may be the result of whatever has deformed them. There is evidence that at least some of the glass was cylinder-blown, a technique in which the glass was blown into an elongated cylindrical bubble, then cut along its length, opened out and flattened in the furnace (also known as 'broad; or 'muff' glass). The edges were slightly rounded (as seen on Fig. 36.219 and 238 (not shown)), and the sheet varied in thickness and had a slightly uneven surface. A number of fragments below have a significant difference in the thickness of the glass, and some fragments are noticeably uneven, appearing slightly bent (e.g. Fig. 33.50, 69).

White window glass was made in England, in medieval forest glasshouses such as those excavated in the Surrey/Sussex Weald, which are documented from c.1240 and known to have supplied window glass to royal chapels at Westminster and Windsor (Tyson, 2000, 7-8). Less evidence is available for other glasshouses that would have operated around in England, but they include a reference to tenants of a glasshouse in Inglewood Forest, Cumbria, including John Vitriarius in 1317 (Parker, 1909, 35). Glasshouses were also operating in medieval Staffordshire probably from the 13th century onwards, with documentary evidence as well as the excavation of a 14th century glass furnace (Tyson, 2000, 8). Higher quality crown glass was sometimes imported from Normandy, but it is most likely that the Holme Cultram glass was all English. It is known that glaziers from York worked in Cumbria from the early 14th century onwards (Allen, 2009b).

The heavily pitted condition of the exterior surfaces of the grisaille suggests that the glass remained *in situ* until the Dissolution in 1538. It is likely that the windows were subsequently removed and deliberately stripped for their lead cames, discarding the less valuable glass, as is thought to have occurred at Battle Abbey in Sussex. At Battle, 13th century grisaille glass was found in the reredorter area, thought to have been removed from the chapter house, and removed to the 'more convenient' reredorter to strip the lead off (Kerr, 1985, 128). At Holme Cultram the majority of the glass came from Trench 3, the reredorter area, with smaller quantities from other areas of the abbey including No. 179 (Fig. 35) from the chapter house area. Excavations of other Cistercian sites have found glass from the abbey churches at Bordesley in Worcestershire, Newminster in Northumberland and Warden in Bedfordshire, from the refectories at Hailes in Gloucestershire and Kirkstall in Yorkshire, and the room over the chapter house at Calder in Cumbria (Marks, 1993, 136). The distribution of the Holme Cultram glass cannot confirm in which buildings it was originally situated.

St. Bernard of Clairvaux, founder of the Cistercian movement, instructed against the use of colour figures and images in window glass (Allen, 2009). The first Cistercian window designs were geometric patterns of unpainted quarries known as 'grisaille'; this developed into a version with painted geometric vegetal designs, still largely using colourless glass but sometimes punctuated with coloured quarries. Painted vegetation

was 'thought to represent Christ the Creator symbolising truth, the Resurrection and the Tree of Jesus' (Allen, 2009a).

The painted glass of Holme Cultram covered a total area of 1323cm², slightly more than the unpainted glass (see below), but still only enough survives to fill a panel c. 40x33cm. In keeping with its Cistercian character, it consisted largely of early to mid-13th century grisaille designs on greenish-colourless (known as 'white') glass. This distinctive and repetitive style is relatively easy to identify from small fragments even if the exact design cannot be reconstructed. A much smaller quantity of painted glass likely to date to the 14th and 15th centuries was more difficult to attribute to a particular subject or date as it was comprised only of tiny fragments of more complex and diverse designs.

The general design of the grisaille windows at Holme Cultram was probably something like the complete early 13th century windows seen at Lincoln and Salisbury Cathedrals and Westminster Abbey (Marks, 1993, 131, Fig.102 a-c). Typically, an overall geometric design emanates from a central motif (sometimes with fleur-de-lys corners as Fig. 33. 66) with circular or square banded frames surrounding it, filled with curving vegetal stems and 'stiff-leaf' foliage decoration. The vegetal grisaille design differs in the arrangement of stems, a cross-hatched or plain background, and there may or may not be fruits, or coloured quarries punctuating the white glass. Different border designs are used and there may be a variant vegetal design in wide border panels down the edges.

Design types A-G of the Holme Cultram glass showed 'stiff-leaf' foliage, some with veins and shading along one side of the stem, but others lacked veins. Many had a cross hatched background, but not all, and there were indications that some foliage may have had fruits. The foliage and stems varied in scale, with some extremely narrow stems and small foliage, while other stems were much wider with larger foliage lobes. There was some evidence of interlacing stems (e.g. Fig. 32.40). Grisaille designs may have had geometric straps or bands of plain glass within the design, as at Lincoln or Auxerre (Marks, 1993, 132, Fig. 103). This was generally regarded as more of a Continental feature, whereas English windows were more likely to have had a small edge of plain glass (*Ibid.*, Fig. 102a,c). Some, but not all of the plain glass fragments from Holme Cultram showed that they came from rectangular quarries. Other fragments included a quatrefoil, and a dotted circle which may have punctuated the window. Borders that were contemporary with the grisaille included beading, consisting of a row of large or small plain circles, or dotted circles (border designs Fig. 31.1-3) and six-petalled flowers painted along an edge (Fig. 36.219). More detailed descriptions of each style can be found below.

The Holme Cultram grisaille is typical of fragments found in excavations of other religious foundations of that date, both Cistercian and other orders across Europe. They include Battle and Bayham Abbeys in the south east (Kerr, 1983 and 1985), Eynsham Abbey in Oxfordshire (Cropper, 2003) and Garendon Abbey (Cistercian) near Loughborough (Leicester Museum collections). This glazing style was also popular in cathedrals, particularly Lincoln, Salisbury, York, Westminster Abbey, and the Corona Chapel at Canterbury. As well as being cheaper than the coloured glass designs that had preceded it, it transmitted more light. This style was common from the early to mid-13th century.

By the end of the 13th and into the 14th century more naturalistic forms of foliage were used in window designs, painted on plain backgrounds and still known as grisaille. Examples with cursively painted oak leaves and more detailed veining can be seen in York Minster chapter house c. 1285-90 (Marks, 1993, 147, Fig. 117) and in the grisaille background to figurative coloured panels at Merton College, Oxford c. 1290s (window N4;wwwtherosewindow.com). Seven fragments from Holme Cultram are likely to come from this later type of grisaille, No. 164 (Fig. 34) showing it most clearly.

A number of fragments were painted with designs not characteristic of grisaille. The glass was generally thinner, and had weathered differently with a glassy core and flaky opaque surface weathering, suggesting a slightly different glass composition. They were small fragments, and a few show elements of 14th or 15th century design motifs, the more diverse and complex designs of windows of this date make it much more difficult to identify them from fragments. There were no indications of inscriptions from any fragments, and unlikely to be any figures perhaps other than No. 180 (Fig. 35) which may possibly represent curling hair. No. 170 (Fig. 35) may be part of an architectural canopy typical of those found in the 14th century, which may imply there was a figure below. Nos. 174 and 177 (Fig. 35) show plants with three stems fanning out from the base, comparable to plants found in 15th century window designs, often as background to figures. A few fragments had shading on the exterior surface, which may be backpainting or silver stain, introduced to England in the 14th century. While these fragments suggest a small scale of new glazing in the 14th and 15th centuries, the wider designs remain unknown. From the glass fragments that have survived, we cannot know whether the abbey at Holme Cultram complied with St. Bernard's instructions right through the medieval period. By the 15th century many Cistercian foundations had relaxed and commissioned windows with figures in them. For example, part of an angel of late 15th century style has been excavated from the Cistercian abbey at Furness in Lancashire (Allen, 2009b). The 303 fragments of unpainted window glass came to a total area of 1248cm², approximately the size of a c. 40x31cm pane. Like the painted glass, a significant quantity was weathered opaque brown and c. 3mm thick, probably contemporary with the early grisaille. Other glass was translucent greenish-colourless or had partial opaque surface weathering, generally less than 2mm thick. There were examples of fragments with flame- smoothed edges, either right in the corner of a quarry, or along a straight or slightly curved edge. The relatively small amount of plain glass suggests that it may represent unpainted areas within or around the painted windows, rather than completely plain windows.

Description of design types found at Holme Cultram

Design types A-G: Vegetal grisaille (early to mid 13ᵗʰ century)

This general style incorporates stiff-leaf foliage, predominantly with trefoil lobes, painted in bold lines usually with a cross-hatched background but sometimes plain, with veining or shading on the stems, or with 'spurs' at the join between the foliage and the stem. It is likely that all fragments within A-G were part of the same scheme; the different elements of the design are grouped separately below since there were subtle differences in styles. The paint is a red-brown tone, sometimes standing slightly proud of the surface. The majority of the fragments are thick (c. 3mm) weathered brown and opaque. Four fragments are greatly misshapen, perhaps through heat distortion, and now appear opaque pale blue or blue-green. Other fragments are slightly bent. Most of the border fragments were probably also part of the general grisaille glazing scheme.

Design type A: Vegetal stiff-leaf grisaille with cross-hatched backgrounds and veining

(Nos. 1-13, Fig. 31) *16 fragments, area 99cm2*

These fragments show boldly painted vegetal stems and foliage with cross-hatched backgrounds and veining on stems, on thick, opaque weathered glass. No.1 is the best preserved example, with a wide main stem with a vein on one side, and a side stem ending in a trefoil. No. 4 shows spurs from the join between the stem and foliage. No. 10 has a wide stem that appears to be shaded and has a vein along one side. Veins and shadings are shown along both sides of the stem on No. 13, while No. 2 shows a thin vein down part of the middle of a stem. Cross-hatching of various different scales is found, larger scale on No. 8, and finer on No. 6. The general foliage type is similar to that found at the church of Stanton St. John, Oxfordshire (CVMA 020935) and Lincoln Cathedral (CVMA 010034).

Design type B: Vegetal stiff-leaf grisaille with cross-hatched background, no visible veining

(Nos. 17-49, Fig. 32) *33 fragments, area 167cm²*

These are similar to the designs above, but without visible veining. In many cases this may be because the fragments are small, and grisaille stems were often only partially veined. No. 40 is a larger quarry where there is still no apparent veining. Some have wide stems and larger foliage lobes (No. 34), while other examples are small with stems only 5mm wide (No. 35). Vegetal grisaille with cross-hatched backgrounds is found with veining in some stems but not necessarily all; for example the Corona Chapel at Canterbury Cathedral shows veins along the stems on the border sections, but on the main foliage there are no veins, only spurs at the junction between the stem and foliage (CVMA 010063). Fragments both with and without veining are found at Battle Abbey (Kerr, 1985). No. 40 shows the stems interlacing, which can also be seen in part of an early 13th century window at Salisbury Cathedral (Marks, 1993, 131, Fig. 102b) and the mid 13th century Five Sisters window at Salisbury Cathedral (Marks, 1993,133, Fig. 105) All opaque, thick glass. Most but not all were from Trench 3.

Design type C: Vegetal grisaille with veining, plain unpainted or matt black background
(Nos. 50-60, Fig. 33) *11 fragments, area 65cm²*

A few fragments show stems with veins, but without the cross-hatched background of type A. This may simply be because the background areas are missing on these fragments, although No. 30 appears to have a plain background behind the foliage, and grisaille is also found with foliage on plain backgrounds (e.g. Selling, Kent). No. 50 is rare in this assemblage, showing several veins on three large foliage lobes/petals, also found on the foliage trefoils at Selling church. Veined foliage is shown in combination with plain foliage on 13th century grisaille, for example at Salisbury (Marks 1993, 131, Fig. 102b). Veined foliage on a matt black background was found amongst the 13th century fragments at Battle Abbey (Kerr 1985, 129, Fig. 40. 11-13). All thick opaque fragments.

Design type D: Vegetal grisaille with plain background and no visible veining
(Nos. 61-2, Fig. 33) *2 fragments, area 14cm²*

Two fragments of small trefoils were found with no veining and plain background areas behind. They are consistent with the general grisaille designs already discussed.

Design type E: Other elements of 13th century grisaille design
(Nos. 63-70, Fig. 33)

Circular fruits next to stiff-leaf foliage design (may have cross-hatching in background)
(Nos. 63-65, Fig. 33) *3 fragments, area 15cm²*

Three fragments can be identified as having parts of circular fruits Nos. 63 and 64 having a cross-hatched background, and No. 64 having a cross-hatched background, and No. 64 probably part of a cluster of at least five fruits. Clusters of fruits are common next to the foliage of stiff-leaf vegetal grisaille, for example in clusters of three at the church of Stanton St. John, Oxfordshire CVMA 020935) and Canterbury Cathedral Corona Chapel. (CVMA 010063), while Salisbury Cathedral has larger clusters of fruits (Marks, 1993, 131, Fig. 102b). One fragment with three fruits was found at Battle Abbey (Kerr, 1985, 129, Fig. 40.14) and fragments with three fruits and cross-hatched backgrounds at Bayham Abbey (Kerr, 1983, 62, Fig. 16.26-7).

Square bordered design with fleur-de-lys leaves on quatrefoil, central circle and veins
(No.66, Fig. 33) *4 adjoining fragments area 15cm²*

No.66 shows part of a design in a probable square bordered quarry, with a small square in the centre, four circles and veins surrounding it, and one surviving corner showing a fleur-de-lys design. This is likely to come from similar to the centre of a grisaille design, such as that in a square bordered quarry, at Salisbury Cathedral (Marks, 1993, 131, Fig. 102b). This also has a quatrefoil design with leaves in the form of a fleur-de-lys in each corner, and a central circle with veins leading out from it. The four circles surrounding the centre are formed by the turn between the four 'fleur-de-lys' leaves, as are the circles between the four leaves of a rosette on a yellow quarry in the centre of a window dating to c. 1230 at Lincoln Cathedral (Brown, 1994, 58). A fragment of a similar design was found amongst the 13th century grisaille at Battle Abbey (Kerr, 1985, 129 & 131, No.17).

Other grisaille motifs
(Nos. 67-70, Fig. 33) *4 fragments, area 17cms²*

A small circular quarry No. 68 shows a circular painted border and a dot in the centre, similar to the rows of dotted circles in Border Style 3. Similar single dotted circles are seen within quarries punctuating the 13th century grisaille at the church of Stanton St. John, Oxfordshire (CVMA 020935). The device is in keeping with the grisaille style, as is No.69, which shows a bold painted quatrefoil. Quatrefoils on cross-hatched backgrounds are seen in border sections of grisaille windows such as Lincoln (CVMA 010034). No. 70, a small fragment has a matt area with some 'c's picked out of it, and an unpainted area with some fine lines along one side, and bears some resemblance to the wing and breast of birds such as those seen in a grisaille window of c. 1270 at Bradwell Abbey (Marks, 1993, 155, Fig. 124), but is too small to be conclusive. Finally, No. 67 is a heat-distorted fragment, now opaque pale blue-green in colour, which shows the remains of a bold outline of a number of petals or foliage lobes. Again, this is consistent with a grisaille style.

Design type F: Cross-hatched background, may have edge of bold lines from grisaille designs
(Nos. 71-87, Fig. 34) *17 fragments, area 55cm²*

These fragments could come from any of the grisaille styles A-B or E above.

Design type G: Other fragments with bold curving or angular lines consistent with 13th century grisaille design
(Nos. 88-161, Fig. 34) *74 fragments, area 248cm²*

These fragments are consistent with the grisaille discussed above, but not enough survives to assign them to a particular subcategory.

Design type H: Oak- leaf grisaille. Fine lines with veins and plain background (late 13th or early 14th century)
(Nos. 162-169, Fig. 34) *8 fragments, area 39cm²*

By the end of the 13th century more naturalistic forms of foliage were used in window designs, continuing into the early 14th century. No. 164 shows veined leaves resembling oak leaves, which are smaller and more finely and cursively painted than the earlier designs. The stems lead off a circle, and have a plain background. Six further fragments are probably part of the same design. They resemble the leaves found in York Minster chapter house c. 1285-90 (Marks, 1993, 147, Fig. 117), and in the grisaille background to figurative coloured panels in window N4 at Merton College, Oxford, c. 1290s. These are all more naturalistic, veined, and on plain backgrounds.

Design type I: Motifs not attributable to early grisaille types (possibly 14th or 15th century designs)
(Nos. 170-201, Fig. 35) *32 fragments area 174cm²*

A number of fragments had designs different to the characteristic 13th century grisaille above. Many were also thinner glass, with a flakey opaque surface weathering but still greenish-colourless glass inside. They are generally small fragments, and part of more diverse and complex designs than the grisaille, making them difficult to attribute to a particular style or date. Some can be compared to the motifs found in the 14th and 15th centuries.

Architectural
(No. 170, Fig. 35) *1 fragment, area 14cms²*

No. 170 shows two lines coming to a point, with a cusp pointing outward on one, which has some resemblance to canopies or other architectural elements in 14th century figurative designs, e.g. Marks, 1993, 164, Fig. 133, *c.* 1350-60 Gloucester Cathedral; ibid, 155, Fig.124, *c.* 1325-40 Stanford on Avon.

Shapes within matt painted area

(Nos. 171-3, Fig. 35) *3 fragments, area 11cm²*

Nos. 171-2 show a small 'fleur-de-lys' shape, and small trefoil motif left unpainted (or picked out) on a matt painted background. These are not typical of the main grisaille design, but are more likely to come from border sections contemporary with the grisaille, or later figurative windows. No. 173 has irregular wavy lobed edges to two areas of matt paint , also seen as background in figurative designs, which are unlikely to have been found in a Cistercian abbey until the 14th or 15th century.

Plant and floral motifs

(Nos. 174-8, Fig. 35) *5 fragments, area 21cm²*

No. 174 is clearly a picked-out plant, with three stems fanning out, on a matt background, similar to the fragments above. The plant style is similar to those on an early 15th century window at All Saints, York (Marks, 1993, 181, Fig. 146), although those plants are painted on a plain background. No. 177 also shows a plant with three stems fanning out from the base, with additional stems to either side with crossing fronds, which are very similar to those on a fragment excavated at Bayham Abbey and thought to be a 15th century background floral design (to a figure) (Kerr, 1983, 66 & 69, Fig. 20, no.101). No. 178 shows two small petals with very finely painted veins, similar to a number of 15th century flower designs (e.g. church East Harling, Norfolk; therosewindow. com). No.176 has a larger petal/foliage lobe with a lobed edge, and No. 175 again has two petals or foliage lobes with veins, and a matt painted background.

Arches and rays

(No. 179, Fig. 35) *1 fragment, area 14cms²*

No. 179 is a relatively large fragment, showing an overlapping scale design of curved lines next to a straight border, with rows of thin lines within each of the larger 'arches'. The exterior has signs of possible shading or silver stain, and the thinly painted lines make it unlikely to be the early 13th century grisaille; it could be contemporary with the later oak leaf grisaille (type H).

Fine cursive painted lines

(Nos. 180-181, Fig. 35) *2 fragments, area 7cm²*

Nos. 180-1 have very fine painted cursive curling lines. Those on 180 are tight curls, with indications of some picked out on top possibly hair, and is the only possible fragment that may be part of a figure, although this is by no means certain.

Miscellaneous

(Nos. 182-201, Fig. 35) *20 fragments area 116cm²*

Various other fragments show painted designs not typical of grisaille, but too small to identify what glazing scheme they may come from. They include finely painted lines, irregular painted shapes, and three close straight parallel lines crossing between two border lines (No.188).

J Border designs

(Nos. 202-219, Fig. 36) *18 fragments, area 55cm²*

(Nos. 207, 211, 216, 218, Fig. 36, *likely to be later, various dates, probably mostly 13th century*)

The border designs identified at Holme Cultram are mainly on narrow rectangular c.11-16mm. wide. Similar sized qurries are known from Battle Abbey (Kerr, 1985, 131, Border Design

11) but this also had much wider quarries, 47mm, showing quatrefoils on a cross-hatched background, part of the early 13th century grisaille style (Kerr, 1985, 129, Border Design I). There may be other glass from Holme Cultram that came from larger borders, but which is too fragmented to identify as such.

Border style 1, plain beading, large circles
(Nos. 202-3, Fig. 36) *2 fragments, area 8cm²*

Border style 2, small-scale beading
(Nos. 204-6, Fig. 36) *3 fragments, area 4cm²*

Border style 3, beading with dots in the centre
(Nos. 207-12, Fig. 36) *6 fragments, area 15cm²*

Border style 4, circles picked out of painted background with tiny picked out circles/dots between
(Nos. 213-216, Fig. 36) *4 fragments, area 11cm²*

The most common border style at Holme Cultram is beading in arrow of circles, which may be large plain circles picked out of the paint (Style 1), or variants consisting of small circles (Style 2), or circles with dots in the centre (Style 3). The general style is found as early as the mid-12th century at Chartres Cathedral, such as the Childhood of Christ window in the west front, which includes borders of plain beading on coloured glass, and the smaller-scale beading with a plain band of unpainted glass down one side (Brisac, 1986,15). Style 1 can be seen in England from the end of the 12th–early-13th century in the east window of the Corona Chapel in Canterbury (CVMA 010079), but continues through the period. Style 1 is also found amongst the grisaille fragments at Battle Abbey (Kerr, 1985, 129 & 13, Fig. 40, No. 15). Style 3 is also found from the mid-12th century onwards, seen clearly in Le Mans Cathedral (Brisac, 1986, 23).

A related design has circular lines picked out of a matt background, with small circles or dots between (Style 4).

Border style 5, picked-out zigzag design with dots in between
1 fragment, area 2cm²

Border design 6, diamond surrounded by four small dots, border within larger fragment
(No. 218, Fig. 36) *1 fragment, area 6cm²*

Another general style found in the Corona Chapel, Canterbury, and at Holme Cultram is a zigzag design picked out of the paint (Style 5; CVMA 010063). Design 6 is a border with painted diamonds, which is part of a larger quarry rather than a separate border quarry, and may be later in date; the glass is thinner with opaque surfaces.

Border style 7, painted flowers within borderline
(No. 219, Fig. 36) *1 fragment, area 9cm²*

Finally, one fragment has two six-petalled flowers with circular centres alongside an edge with painted borderline, and possible shading or silver stain on the exterior (Style 7). Painted quatrefoil flowers are commonly found in grisaille borders (e.g. Corona Chapel, Canterbury, CVMA 010252), so this design would be consistent with grisaille.

K Fragments with parts of straight and curved lines, date uncertain
(Nos. 220-61, Fig. 36) *42 fragments, area 194cm²*

This category overlaps with G in being miscellaneous straight and curved painted lines on the fragments, but the glass itself differs from the thick, opaque weathered type which most of the 13th century grisaille designs are found on. It is generally thinner or has very heavy flaky opaque surfaces with a greenish-colourless core, suggesting it might be later. Three fragments have traces on the exterior surface that might be silver stain, introduced to England in the 14th century. The date of the fragments is uncertain from their appearance, although some fragments may be contemporary with Type H on which the later oak leaf grisaille style are found. The lines include border lines as well as other undiagnostic designs.

I Painted fragments, but indistinct paint and undiagnostic designs
62 fragments, area 166cm²

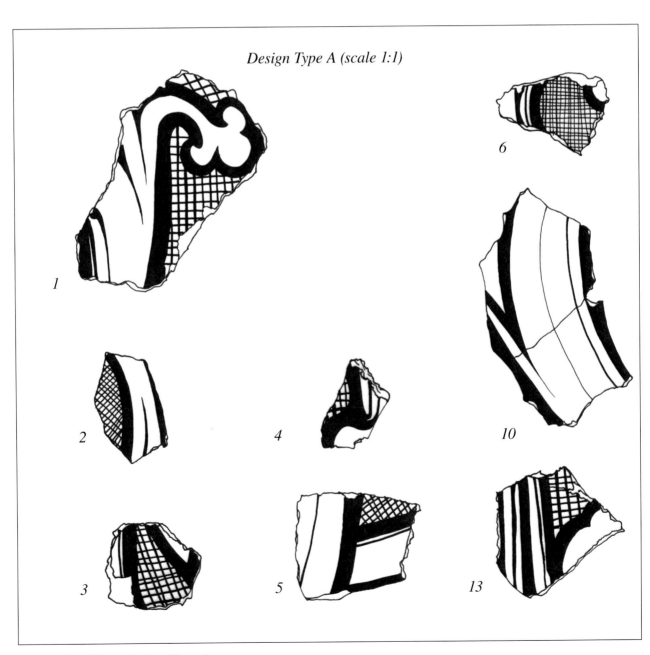

Design Type A (scale 1:1)

Figure 31: Glass design Type A

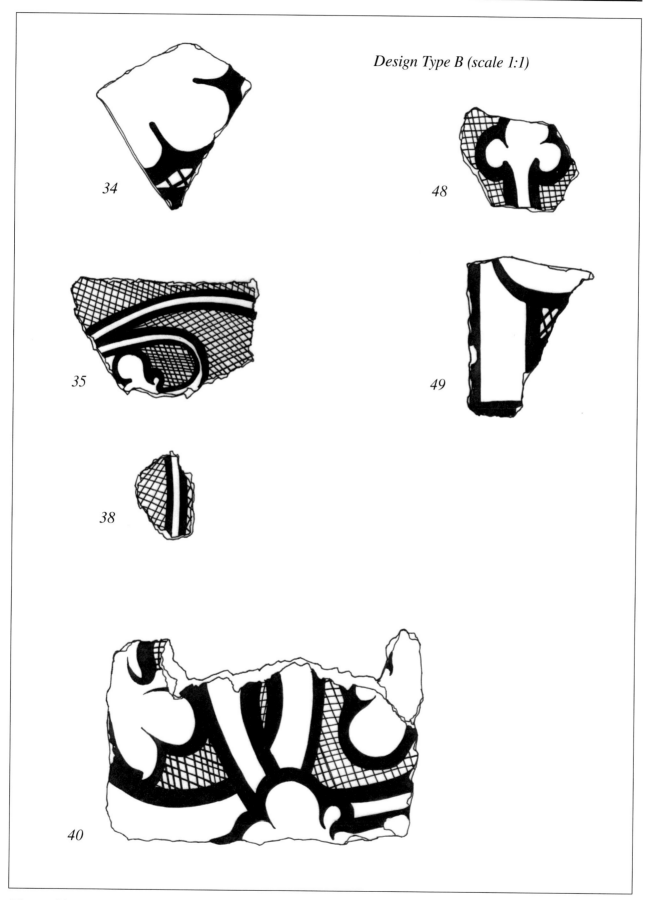

Figure 32: Glass design Type B

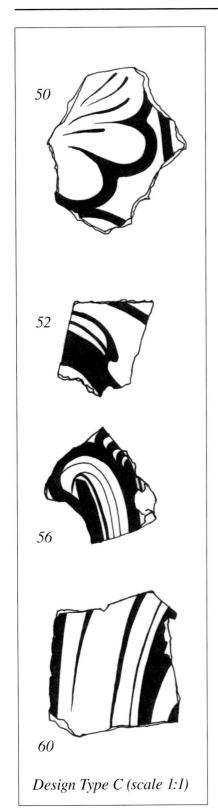

50

52

56

60

Design Type C (scale 1:1)

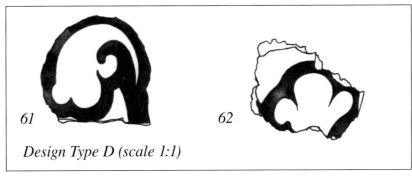

61

62

Design Type D (scale 1:1)

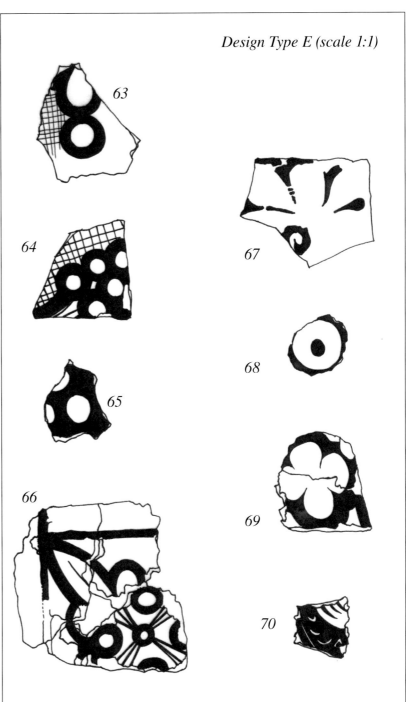

Design Type E (scale 1:1)

63

64

65

66

67

68

69

70

Figure 33: Glass design Types C, D and E

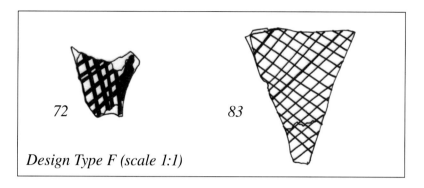

Design Type F (scale 1:1)

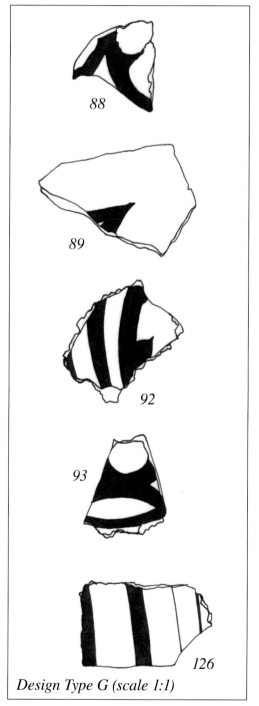

Design Type G (scale 1:1)

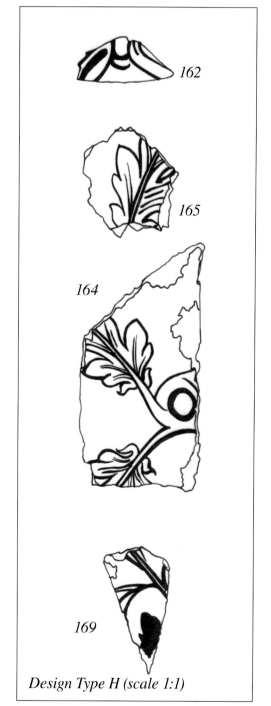

Design Type H (scale 1:1)

Figure 34: Glass design Types F, G and H

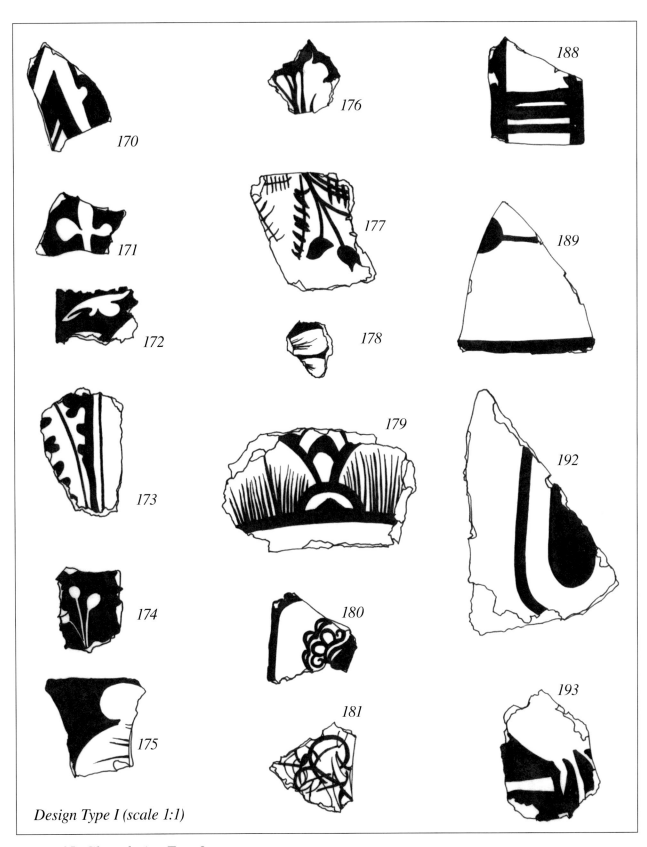

Design Type I (scale 1:1)

Figure 35: Glass design Type I

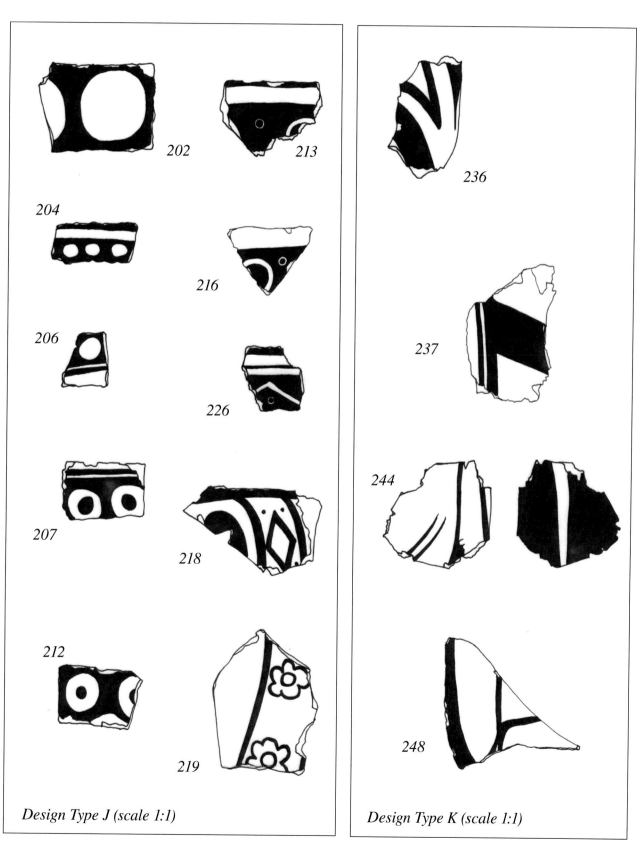

Design Type J (scale 1:1)

Design Type K (scale 1:1)

Figure 36: Glass design Types J and K

The Pottery,

by Thomas Mace and Jo Dawson
(for catalogue, see pages 83-87)

A total of 1419 individual pottery fragments were recovered potentially ranging in date from the late 12th to the 20th century. The majority came from stratified deposits and only 41 sherds (2·9%) could not be allocated to a specific context. For the purposes of this report post-medieval pottery is generally considered to be that with a date-range beginning in at least the 17th century, however, early brown-glazed red earthenwares and Blackwares (including Cistercian ware) have potential origins in the 15th century or, in the case of the non-factory-produced stonewares, in the 14th century. In general only small parts of post-medieval vessel profiles were available but a good range of finewares and coarsewares is present (see Table 3 and Table 4). The earlier medieval ware-types, which were introduced elsewhere in the region perhaps in the late 12th and 13th century, include lightly gritted / sandy wares, partially reduced and reduced wares. A summary of the analysis report is presented here (for the full report see Medieval pottery accounts for 49·4% of the overall assemblage by sherd count (Table 1). Fragments of the earliest material in particular are small and much abraded, indicative of some post-depositional disturbance, and the number of refitting fragments generally is relatively low. Although the majority of the medieval pottery comprises body sherds there are 33 rim fragments, 27 handle fragments (excluding those which are attached to part of a rim), 40 bases, and fragments of the bungholes of three cisterns represented within the assemblage. Few vessels could be reconstructed, although those that could be identified seem to represent functional and utilitarian items. The earlier material is dominated by jars and/or cooking pots and there is a wider range of forms present amongst the later wares, including jugs and bunghole cisterns.

'Firing faults' are also present on some vessels. Similar vessel forms have been illustrated from comparative medieval assemblages elsewhere in the region (e.g., McCarthy and Brooks 1988, 1992; Kendal: Whitehead et al forthcoming) and more locally (*Carlisle:* Jope and Hodges 1956; Jarrett and Edwards 1964; Brooks 1999, 2000, 2010; Bradley and Miller 2009).

The Medieval fabrics

The medieval pottery was analysed following guidelines provided by the *Medieval Pottery Research Group* (1998, 2001) and a fabric series was devised following the *Guidelines for the Processing and Publication of Medieval Pottery from Excavations* (Blake and Davey, 1983) and Pottery in Archaeology (Orton et al, 2008). All the vessels appear to have been wheel-thrown and glazes tend to be thin and smooth. A summary of the fabrics which were identified within the assemblage is presented here and a full description of each fabric is available in the analysis report (Greenlane Archaeology 2011). These fabrics are more typically grouped by their common names, or 'ware types', and include lightly gritted / sandy and fine wares and Partially Reduced and Reduced Grey wares (e.g., McCarthy and Brooks, 1992; Brooks, 1999, 2000, 2010; Bradley and Miller, 2009; see Table 2). The suggested date ranges for these wares are approximate, based on general typological considerations and parallels elsewhere in the region (e.g., McCarthy and Brooks, 1992), perhaps most especially Carlisle (Brooks, 1999, 2000; Bradley and Miller, 2009), but comparative analysis is hampered by local fabric reference collections being unavailable.

The medieval assemblage is dominated by Reduced Grey wares (sometimes referred to as the 'Reduced Green ware' tradition (Brooks 1999, 103; 2000, 140)) (see Table 2), which potentially date from the late 13th to the early

Ware type	Sherd count	% by sherd count
Lightly gritted / sandy wares	158	11.1
Partially reduced wares	129	9.1
Reduced wares	414	29.2
Post-medieval coarsewares	408	28.8
Post-medieval finewares	310	21.8

Table 1: Ware types by sherd count

17th century (*Carlisle*: Brooks, 1999, 103, 2000, 140; Bradley and Miller, 2009, 664; *Kendal*: Whitehead et al, forthcoming; *Penrith*: Newman et al, 2000, 123), with the bulk of the Reduced material likely to date from the late 14th to 15th century (Miller pers comm.). The earlier lightly gritted and sandy material is much rarer, with a suggested date range from the late 12th to 14th century (McCarthy and Brooks, 1992; *Carlisle*: Bradley and Miller, 2009, 663-664; Brooks, 1999, 103; 2000, 140; *Kendal*: Whitehead et al, forthcoming; *Penrith*: Newman et al, 2000, 122), which potentially overlaps with the period of circulation of the Partially Reduced and Reduced Grey ware traditions around the late 13th to 14th century (McCarthy and Brooks, 1992, 34; *Carlisle*: Brooks, 2000, 140; cf. *Kendal*: Whitehead et al, forthcoming; *Penrith*: Newman et al, 2000, 122). Very few fragments show any sign of decoration (only 19 fragments show decoration, which accounts for around 2·7% of the assemblage by sherd count) and only a small number of pieces of the more unusual fabrics were recovered, including a small quantity of possibly imported wares, comprising six fragments of a yellow ware (Sandy Fabric 4) and 12 fragments of off-white sandy fabrics (Sandy Fabric 6), accounting for less than 2·6% of the assemblage by sherd count. The assemblage notably does not contain any gritty ware,

which dominates 12th and early 13th century assemblages in the region (McCarthy and Brooks, 1992, 22; *Penrith*: Newman et al, 2000, 120-121; *Carlisle*: Brooks, 1999, 102; 2000, 139; *Kendal*: Whitehead et al, forthcoming).

Lightly Gritted / Sandy and fine wares (Sandy Fabrics 1-8)

Eight principal sandy fabrics and one possible sub-fabric were identified, which varied from very fine almost powdery to hard fabrics, and ranged from light oranges to shades of grey in section, with sparse to moderate fine to very fine inclusions. Glazes were most commonly applied externally and on the whole varied from light yellowish- to dark greens to splashy orangey-brown to darker reddish-brown. Sandy Fabrics 4 and 6 are unusual: Sandy Fabric 4 is a light pinkish-white to buff fabric with a fairly uniform yellow glaze and Sandy Fabric 6 varies from a very pale pinkish-white to almost white in section, often with a laminated effect, and less frequently the core is reduced to grey. The low incidence of Sandy Fabric 6 in particular makes further sub-division of the material unreliable although it might be possible to more satisfactorily sub-divide the material with direct in-hand comparison to material from the areas suggested where it may have originated.

71

Sherd count

Lightly Gritted / Sandy and fine wares	
Sandy Fabric 1	37
Sandy Fabric 2	57
Sandy Fabric 2a	2
Sandy Fabric 3	7
Sandy Fabric 4	6
Sandy Fabric 5	33
Sandy Fabric 6	12
Sandy Fabric 7	3
Sandy Fabric 8	1
Partially Reduced Grey ware	
Partially Reduced Fabric 1	129
Reduced Grey ware	
Reduced Fabric 1	38
Reduced Fabric 2	297
Reduced Fabric 3	79

Table 2: Medieval fabrics by sherd count

Similarities were noted between this group of closely related sandy fabrics and ones which have been recovered from excavations in Carlisle (*fabrics 11, 12, 13, 14, 51, 53*: McCarthy and Brooks, 1992, 28; Brooks, 1999, 103; 2000, 140; 2010, 88; McCarthy and Taylor, 1990, 302), Kendal (Whitehead et al, forthcoming; Miller pers comm.), Cockermouth (Miller pers comm.), Penrith (*fabrics 4 and 5*: Newman et al, 2000, 121-2), and Dacre (*fabrics 3 and 4*: Newman et al, 2000, 121-2) and they likely form part of a lightly gritted / sandy ware tradition of the late 12th to 14th century (McCarthy and Brooks, 1992; e.g., *Carlisle*: Bradley and Miller, 2009, 663-664; Brooks, 1999, 103; 2000, 140; 2010, 88).

A paler variation within Sandy Fabric 6 with a rich copper glaze might originate from the East Coast or possibly from northern Europe (Miller pers comm.) and it certainly shares similarities with *Saintonge*, which is a very high-firing ware, which became common in Chester in the 14th century (Edwards, 2000, 42-3). A decorated fragment is perhaps more similar to material from Dumfriesshire (Miller pers comm.). In descriptive terms, however, it also closely resembles material recovered from Penrith (*fabric 4*: Newman et al, 2000, 121-122) and off-white to buff, lightly gritted, sandy fabrics excavated in Carlisle are also thought to belong to the 'Penrith Buff Sandy ware tradition' and may originate in that area (Brooks, 2010, 88).

Fragments were generally small, although some more sizeable and often refitting pieces were recovered, and fractures tended to be quite abraded due to the relative sandiness of the fabric. Vessel forms were mostly jugs, with side strap handles with an undulating outer surface and emphasised thumb-impressed attachment below the rim and smoothed attachment to the body. The jugs were most likely pear-shaped, with upright rims, sometimes with pinched or pulled lips and flat, obtuse-angled or otherwise slightly sagging bases (Fig. 37.1-20). A uniform glaze was applied externally in most cases, although some fragments are glazed internally as well. One fragment has a 'glaze run', so it is possibly a second (Miller pers comm.). Fragments were generally unembellished although there are rare instances of straight combed lines on the neck and/or shoulder (Fig. 37.5) and nonparallel incised lines on body fragments and non-linear incisions are noted on one body fragment (Fig. 37.18). One much abraded fragment has an applied strip, which has possibly been stabbed or rouletted (Fig. 37.19).

72

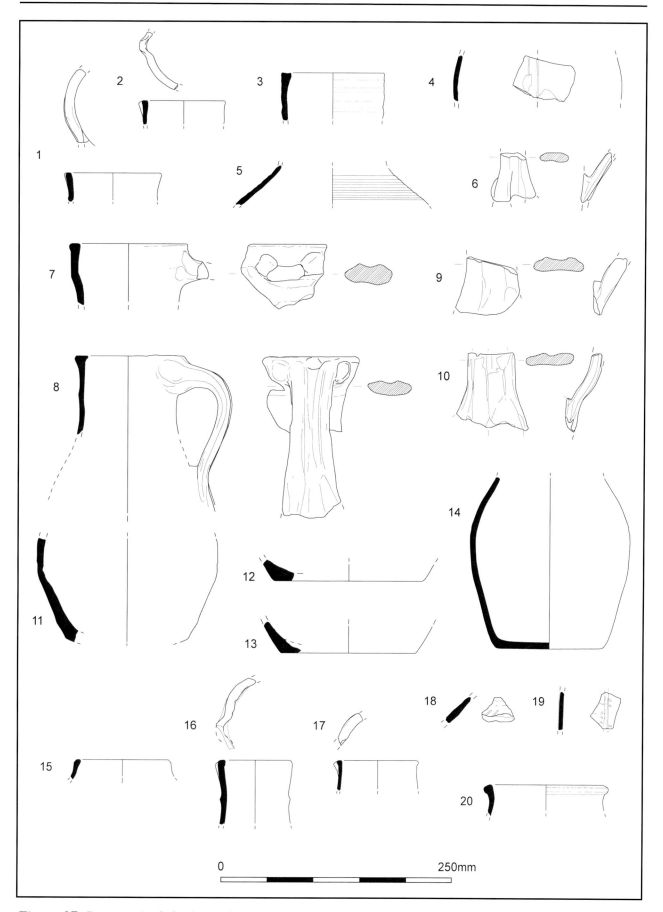

Figure 37: Pottery, Lightly Gritted / Sandy ware vessel forms

Partially Reduced Grey wares
(Partially Reduced Fabric 1)

The vessels comprising this fabric often have heavy ridges on the inner surface from throwing and there are many medium-sized fragments with sharp fractures. The outer surface and most often the outer margin of this hard, lightly gritted sandy fabric is a light grey to buff or whitish colour, usually forming a distinct outer band, while the core tends to be reduced to a slightly darker grey colour and the oxidised inner margins and inner surface vary from a light buff to buff-brown to light reddish-orange colour. The outer surface often has a fairly uniform or less commonly flaking, shiny glaze, which varies from a light apple green to a darker green, sometimes with an unglazed strip externally, but there is no evidence for other surface embellishments. This 'sandwich-effect' cross-section has also been noted generally for three partially reduced fabrics from Carlisle (fabrics 15, 17, and 19) which are often variously lumped together as part of a 'Partially Reduced Grey ware' (e.g., Brooks, 1999, 103; 2000, 140; McCarthy and Brooks, 1992, 24; Bradley and Miller, 2009, 662). These partially reduced fabrics were the dominant ware type of the late 13th to 14th century (McCarthy and Brooks, 1992, 34; *Carlisle*: Brooks, 2000, 140; *Penrith*: Newman et al, 2000, 122).

Most of the smaller more abraded fragments are body sherds from fine, thin-walled vessels, including a globular jug (Fig. 38.21). Other vessels represented were generally jugs with side strap handles with undulating outer surfaces and emphasised thumbed attachments, sometimes with slightly ribbed rims or necks, with upright, simple or slightly thickened rims, with flat, obtuse-angled or slightly sagging bases (Fig. 38.22-32). Firing faults (from stacking) were visible on the undersides of some vessels.

Late Medieval Reduced Grey wares
(Reduced Fabrics 1-3)

The Carlisle Fabric Series lists three Late Medieval Reduced Grey ware fabrics, Fabrics 41, 43, and 45, but these are indistinguishable on the basis of the written descriptions and are effectively a coverall for Late Medieval Reduced Grey ware, which forms part of a widespread northern 'Reduced Green ware' tradition (Brooks, 2010, 89). This became the dominant ware type throughout the region during the 15th and 16th century (*Carlisle*: Brooks, 1999, 103; Bradley and Miller, 2009, 664; *Dacre*: McCarthy and Brooks, 1992, 30; *Kendal*: Whitehead et al forthcoming; *Penrith*: Newman et al, 2000, 123), although a broad date range for the tradition ranges from the late 13th to the early 17th century (*Carlisle*: Brooks, 2000, 140). Three reduced fabrics are represented here all of which have a dense clay matrix with very sparse very fine inclusions. The fabrics are of varying hardness and subtly different colouration, varying from mid to light grey, sometimes with a faintly lighter or very pronounced light grey or whitish outer margin with a dark to very dark grey inner margin and inner surface occasionally with a light-brown to light orangey-brown inner surface. The glaze, which is applied externally, tends to be flaky and varies from light olive to dark green or brown sometimes with a mottled effect.

Often large and refitting fragments of this fabric survive since it tends to be used for large, coarseware vessels, including thick walled jugs and bunghole cisterns (Fig. 38.32-38 and Fig. 39). The vessels usually have simple or slightly thickened rounded upright rims, with pinched lips, and side strap handles with undulating outer surfaces and impressed thumbed termini. Bungholes tend to be smoothed and unembellished, although one example has a slashed vertical line externally (Fig. 39.44) which is also recorded on material excavated

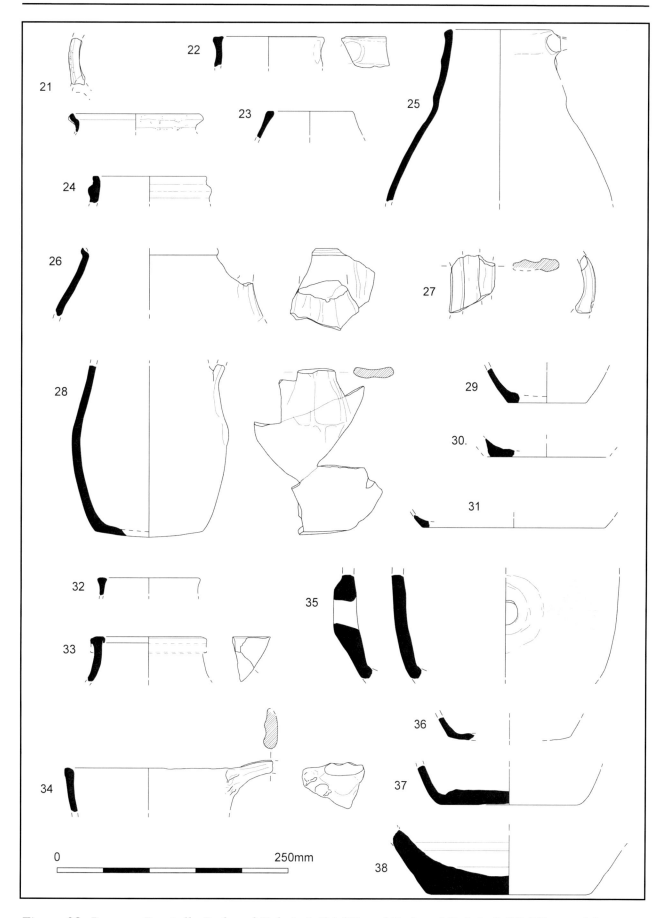

Figure 38: Pottery, Partially Reduced Fabric 1 (21-31) and Reduced Fabric 1 (32-38) vessel forms

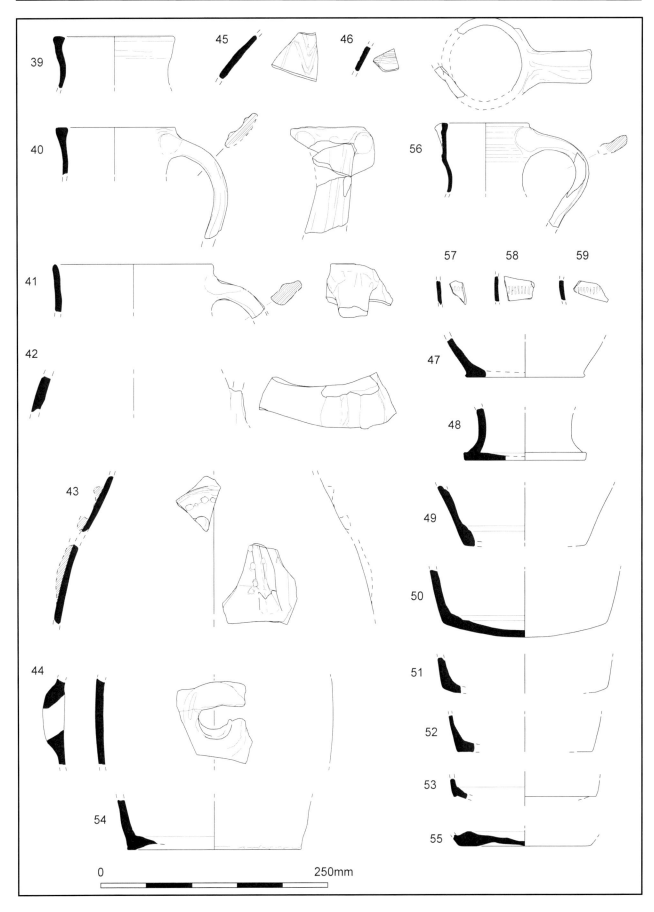

Figure 39: Pottery, Reduced Fabric 2 (39-55) and Reduced Fabric 3 (56-59) vessel forms

in Carlisle (Brooks, 2000, 140). One unusual rim fragment has been rolled on the inside and appears to have been collared on the outside (perhaps with an applied strip decoration, which is now missing) and another has an unusual handle attached that rises above the level of the rim and the strap appears to have been 'pinched' to attach it (Fig. 38.34) rather than leaving a thumbed impression which is more usually the case. Ribbed and/or slightly thickened upright rims are represented and there is one example with a pinched (almost 'pie-crust') rim. Bases are generally flat, obtuse-angled or sagging; there was one slightly recessed, obtuse-angled base (Fig. 39.55), and one splayed flat base of a jug (Fig. 39.48) and one has a thumbed base (Fig. 39.54). There are examples of 'firing faults' from stacking and some of the chunkier base fragments were noted to be particularly crudely made (Miller pers comm.). Examples of decoration included combed straight or wavy pattern lines (Fig. 39.45-46) with very infrequent, isolated incidences of linear incisions on body fragments. Some body fragments appear to have been textured with a faint 'spiralling' or 'wavy'

pattern whereby the outer surface of the vessel has been firmly brushed or gently scored while it was leather hard (i.e., before firing). One vessel has applied strips and stabbed decoration and possibly more than one applied pellet (Fig. 39.43) and three body fragments have square-rilled decoration (at least two if not all of which may be part of the same vessel; see Fig. 39.57-59).

The Post-medieval Pottery

Post-medieval coarseware fabrics

Coarsewares are those with walls thicker than their fineware equivalents and are presented as a separate category to the finewares (see Table 3). The most numerous fabrics, Coarse earthenware Fabrics 1 and 2, comprise mainly utilitarian wares not much influenced by changing fashions, and therefore of little use for accurate dating. However, some of the other coarseware fabrics were in use for far shorter periods of time, and can therefore be dated with similar ease to their fineware versions (e.g., slip-coated ware). Some of the decorated vessels and coarse earthenware vessels from this large assemblage are illustrated in Fig. 40 and Fig. 41.

Ware	Sherd count	Date
Non-factory-produced salt-glazed stoneware	12	14th to mid-18th century
Slipware	10	17th to 19th century
Speckled-glazed buff-coloured earthenware	4	Late 17th to early 18th century?
Slip-coated ware	15	Late 17th to 18th century
Coarse earthenware	324	Late 17th to early 20th century
Glazed red earthenware with white slip-coated interior	34	(Late 18th) 19th to early 20th century
Factory-produced stoneware	9	19th to mid-20th century

Table 3: Post-medieval coarsewares

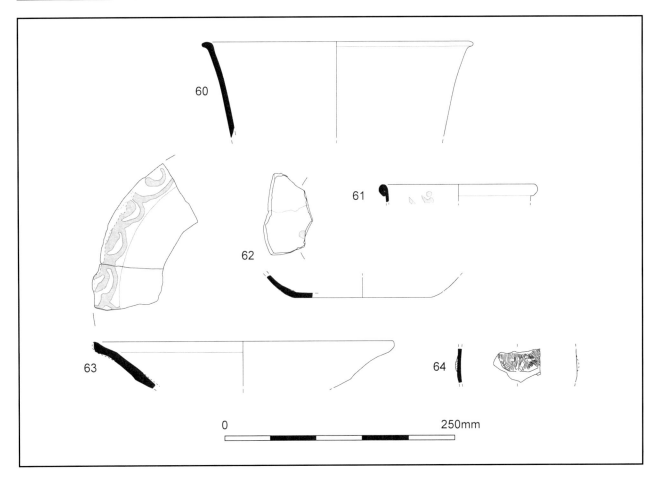

Figure 40: Pottery, Slipped and decorated post-medieval coarseware vessel forms

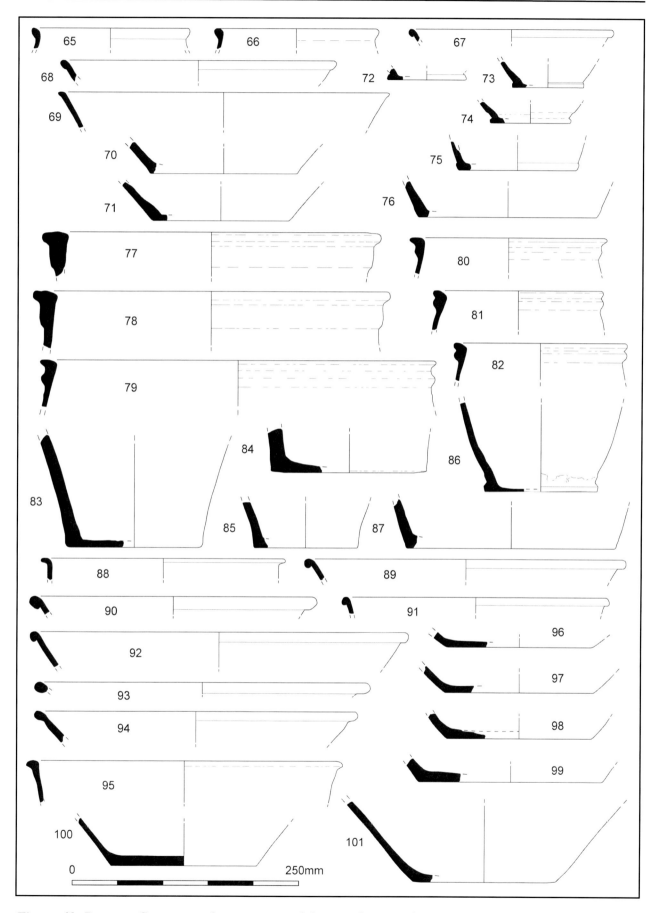

Figure 41: Pottery, Coarse earthenware vessel forms, showing decoration

79

Post-medieval fineware fabrics

Of particular interest amongst the finewares (Table 3) were the early brown-glazed red earthenwares and Blackwares, showing possible developmental stages from medieval pottery fabrics towards Cistercian ware (Table 4).

Ware	Sherd count	Date
Non-factory-produced stoneware	6	14th to mid 18th century
Early brown-glazed red earthenware	13	15th to 18th century
Blackwares (including Cistercian ware)	49	Mid 15th to 18th century
Slipware	13	17th to 19th century
Black-glazed buff-coloured earthenware	4	Late 17th to early 18th century
Speckled-glazed buff-coloured earthenware	1	Late 17th to early 18th century
Fine earthenware	19	Late 17th to early 20th century
Mottledware	2	18th century
Tin-glazed earthenware	5	18th century
Creamware	39	Mid to late 18th century
Glazed black earthenware	2	Mid 18th to 19th century?
Buff-coloured earthenware (factory-produced)	28	Mid 18th to early 20th century
Porcelain	1	Mid 18th to early 20th century?
Creamware / pearlware / white earthenware (burnt)	14	Mid 18th to 20th century
Rockingham-type wares	5	Mid 18th to 20th century
Pearlware	22	Late 18th to early 19th century
Pearlware / white earthenware	1	Late 18th to 19th century
White earthenware	78	Late 18th to early 20th century
Factory-produced stoneware	4	19th to mid 20th century
Bone china	4	19th to 20th century

Table 4: Post-medieval finewares

Early brown-glazed red earthenwares
(Early brown-glazed red earthenware Fabrics 1-2)

Two fabrics were identified within the early brown-glazed red earthenware: Fabric 1 is a low-fired brown-glazed red earthenware with applied white slip dots, rough from high grog content, and vessels often have unusual pinched in non-vertical lines (Fig. 42.105); Fabric 2 is an olive-brown metallic-speckled-glazed red earthenware (Table 4). The Fabric 2 fragments are possibly from a single vessel decorated with an applied cone-shaped clay pellet in the same fabric as the vessel below a horizontal ridge (Fig. 42.107).

Blackwares (including Cistercian ware)
(Blackware Fabrics 1-4)

Four fabrics were identified within the 'Blackware': Fabric 1 is a dark brown-glazed red earthenware with a pitted surface and mid-brown to purple patches, with some metallic speckles; Fabric 2 is a dark brown-glazed red earthenware with metallic speckle, but overall having a dull metallic finish, or areas of dull purple; Fabric 3 is a dark brown-glazed red earthenware without metallic speckles or dull metallic or purple areas, and Fabric 4 is like a fineware version of coarse earthenware Fabric 2 (Table 5). Fragments of Fabric 1 are decorated with a horizontal ridge below the rim and applied white slip (Fig. 42.110) and one vessel has an unusual inverted convex rim (Fig. 42.111). Fabric 2 has two examples of identical applied white slip crosses, rough with high white-firing grog content (Fig. 42.118-119), with similarly rough applied whit.e horizontal stripes on a cup handle (Fig. 42.116), and there is an example of applied white slip discs, with some rough inclusions around the outer edge, either side of a lower handle terminal (Fig. 42.113; similar to Wrenthorpe decoration element type 9 (Moorhouse and Roberts, 1992, 92)), and one has an applied smooth white slip horizontal line with ovals attached, all rouletted (Fig. 42.117). No decorated fragments were found in Fabric 3 or 4. Vessels identified were probably cups.

Interestingly, one has had its edge filed down after the rim had broken so that it could continue to be used (Fig. 42.109).

In terms of the earliest post-medieval pottery, it would appear that Blackware Fabrics 1 and 2 represent Cistercian ware vessels, although in most cases the profile information available is limited. A low sherd to vessel ratio hampered comparison in vessel forms with the established Cistercian ware typologies, however, these are thought to include Cistercian ware Type 1 (including decorated examples; Moorhouse and Roberts, 1992, 111-135). As is to be expected the decorative elements on some of the Cistercian ware are regionally distinct from the far better documented assemblages in Yorkshire and direct parallels for the decorative elements on the Cistercian ware vessels have not currently been identified (e.g., Fig. 42.110, Fig. 42.116 and Fig. 42.117). Early brown-glazed red earthenware Fabric 1 is essentially a lower-fired, oxidised, possibly earlier version of Cistercian ware, in terms of its shape and decoration, and it is possible that this may represent a stage of the illusive development of Cistercian ware that has been assumed to exist. Early brown-glazed red earthenware Fabric 2 is likely to post-date Fabric 1 as it appears in as developed a form as Cistercian ware and indeed the later Blackware and may be contemporary with them instead.

Ware	Fabric	Sherd count	Date
Early brown-glazed red earthenware	Fabric 1: Low-fired brown-glazed red earthenware (slip-decorated)	8	15th to 16th century?
	Fabric 2: Olive-brown metallic-speckled-glazed red earthenware	5	Mid 15th to 18th century
Blackwares (including Cistercian ware)	Fabric 1: Dark brown-glazed red earthenware with pitted surface and mid-brown/purple patches, with some metallic speckles	10	Mid 15th to mid 17th century
	Fabric 2: Dark brown-glazed red earthenware with metallic speckles, overall dull metallic finish, or areas of dull purple	36	Mid 15th to mid 18th century
	Fabric 3: Dark brown-glazed red earthenware without metallic speckles or dull metallic or purple areas	2	Mid 15th to 18th century
	Fabric 4	1	17th to 18th century

Table 5: Early brown-glazed red earthenwares and Blackwares

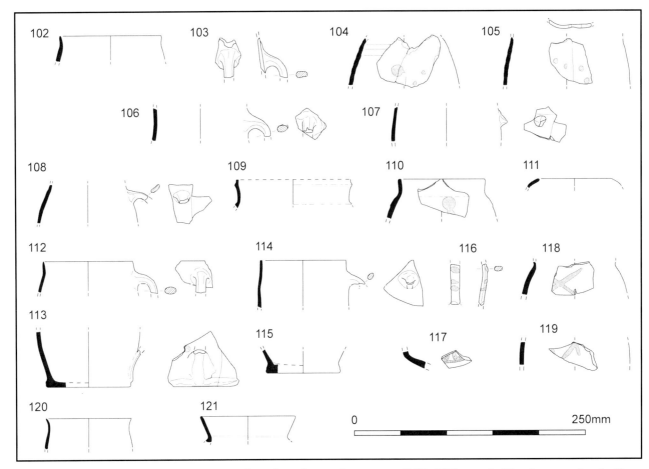

Figure 42: Pottery, Early brown-glazed red earthenware (102-107) and Blackware (including Cistercian ware (108-121) vessel forms and showing decoration

Discussion

The medieval ceramic sequence at Holme Cultram Abbey is broadly similar to excavated material recovered from elsewhere in the region (e.g., McCarthy and Brooks, 1992; Brooks, 2000) and sizeable groups of comparative material have been published from excavations in Carlisle at Blackfriars Street (McCarthy, 1990), St Nicholas Yard (Brooks, 1999), and near the castle (Bradley and Miller, 2009). Unfortunately, medieval ceramics in the north-west of England are, as yet, not understood sufficiently to provide close dating of archaeological deposits (Miller pers comm.) and when pottery types were introduced and when they went out of use is problematic (Brooks, 2000, 139). That many of these wares had a similar or overlapping circulation period is

perhaps not unlikely since the vessel forms are often very alike (which is probably indicative of similar production techniques) and similarities also exist between the fabrics themselves which likely represent a continuum. Given the constraints of the sample size and in the absence of absolute dating evidence to tie to the ceramic sequence, it has not been possible to refine the date of circulation for these wares on the basis of the material recovered. It appears that many of the contexts were mixed in terms of the dates of the material present and in this regard the assemblage is considered of local interest only, fitting as it does within the established sequence of ware types for the area.

The vast majority of the material is assumed to have been derived from local sources. Only a small number of pieces of the more unusual fabrics were recovered, including possible evidence for the importation of some fabrics (e.g., Sandy Fabric 4 and Sandy Fabric 6). Similarly small quantities of off-white sandy fabrics (similar to Sandy Fabric 6) have been recorded from excavations elsewhere in Carlisle and are suggested to have been imports to the area (Brooks, 1999, 103).

The earlier material, represented by the lightly gritted and sandy wares as well as the partially reduced fabrics, appears to have a restricted range of forms dominated by jars and/or cooking pots, which persist potentially from the late 12th to at least the 14th century. There is seemingly a wider range of forms present amongst the Reduced Grey Ware vessels, which are generally thought to be later, including jugs and bunghole cisterns. Overall, decoration is very uncommon within the assemblage and it is usually only present on the Reduced Grey wares and to a lesser extent Sandy Fabrics 1 and 6. Similar decorative techniques have been employed at Carlisle (Brooks, 2000, 140; Bradley and Miller, 2009, 663; Jarrett and Edwards, 1964, 51) and Penrith (Newman et al, 2000, 122) but are applied to different fabrics. It is also worth noting that none of the rim fragments have the

'pie-crust' decoration applied as a secondary process after the wheel-work (also noted in Jope and Hodges, 1956, 102; cf. *Kendal*: Whitehead et al, forthcoming), which is a common technique used elsewhere in the North (e.g., *Silverdale*: White, 2000, 289; *Kendal*: Whitehead et al, forthcoming; noted in Jope and Hodges, 1956, 85). The scarcity of decorated sherds in medieval pottery assemblages is also noted for material excavated nearby in Carlisle (Jope and Hodges, 1956, 102; Brooks 2000, 140; Bradley and Miller, 2009, 663), so perhaps a quality of the pottery in this area at that time is its relative plainness.

Within the post-medieval pottery assemblage the fabrics, forms, and decoration of the early brown-glazed red earthenware, which may represent an early form in the development of Cistercian ware, and the Cistercian ware itself are of particular interest at local and even regional scales. Although only small elements of the individual vessel profiles are present, these nevertheless add to the body of knowledge regarding these 15th to 17th century wares in Cumbria, and possibly also beyond. Unfortunately, it is not clear where these wares were manufactured as direct parallels for some of the decorative elements have so far proved elusive.

Catalogue of illustrated vessels

The fabric and context number is recorded in brackets following the description of each illustration:

1   Simple rim with a pulled lip (Sandy Fabric 1, HC08 (*103*))
2   Simple rim with a pinched pouring lip (Sandy Fabric 1, HC08 (*107*))
3   Ribbed rim thickened externally (Sandy Fabric 1, HC09 EXT (*1047*))
4   Body fragment with nonparallel incised lines (Sandy Fabric 1, HC08 (*107*))
5   Shoulder of a jug with simple combed line decoration (Sandy Fabric 1, HC08 (*107*))
6   Strap handle with an undulating outer surface (Sandy Fabric 1, HC08 (*107*))
7   Thickened rim, probably from a jug, with a thumbed side strap handle (Sandy Fabric 2, HC08 (*101*))
8   Externally thickened and slightly inturned rim of a jug with a thumbed side strap handle, with an undulating outer surface, which flares towards the base (Sandy Fabric 2, HC08 (*189*))
9   Strap handle with an undulating outer surface (Sandy Fabric 2, HC10 TR3 (*44*))
10   Strap handle with an undulating outer surface (Sandy Fabric 2, HC09 (*1001*))

11 Sagging, obtuse-angled base (Sandy Fabric 2, HC10 TR3 (*08*) refitting HC10 TR3 (*09*))

12 Flat, obtuse-angled base (Sandy Fabric 2, HC10 TR3 (*40*))

13 Flat, obtuse-angled base (Sandy Fabric 2, HC10 TR (*07*))

14 Flat, obtuse-angled base of a jug (Sandy Fabric 2, HC08 (*133*))

15 Inturned simple rim (Sandy Fabric 2a, HC10 TR3 (*04*))

16 Upright simple rim with a pinched lip (Sandy Fabric 5, HC10 TR3 (*40*))

17 Upright simple rim with a pinched lip (Sandy Fabric 5, HC10 TR3 (*16*))

18 Shoulder of a jug (?) with non-linear incised decoration (Sandy Fabric 5, HC08 (*100*))

19 Body fragment with applied strip with possible stabbed decoration (Sandy Fabric 6, ?? U/S)

20 Everted, slightly clubbed, rounded rim (Sandy Fabric 8, HC10 TR3 (*37*))

21 Everted and internally bevelled rim of a globular jug with a pulled lip (Partially Reduced Fabric 1, HC09 (*1008*))

22 Upright, externally thickened and slightly inturned rim with thumbed side strap handle (Partially Reduced Fabric 1, HC08 (*103*))

23 Inturned rim, slightly thickened internally (Partially Reduced Fabric 1, HC08 (*100*))

24 Ribbed rim (Partially Reduced Fabric 1, HC08 (*100*))

25 Upright, thickened rim of a jug, with thumbed strap handle terminus (Partially Reduced Fabric 1, HC08 (*103*) refitting HC08 (*106*))

26 Strap handle terminus (Partially Reduced Fabric 1, HC08 (*106*))

27 Strap handle with an undulating outer surface (Partially Reduced Fabric 1, HC08 (*106*))

28 Thumbed terminus of a side strap handle of a jug with a slightly sagging, obtuse-angled base (Partially Reduced Fabric 1, HC10 TR3 (*40*))

29 Flat, obtuse-angled base (Partially Reduced Fabric 1, HC09 (*1022*))

30 Flat, obtuse-angled base (Partially Reduced Fabric 1, HC09 ET2 (*1003*))

31 Flat, obtuse-angled base (Partially Reduced Fabric 1, HC09 (*1012*))

32 Upright, slightly thickened rim (Reduced Fabric 1, HC09 (*1011*))

33 Unusual rim fragment, which appears to have been collared on the outside (perhaps with an applied strip decoration, now missing) and rolled on the inside (Reduced Fabric 1, HC08 (*120*))

34 Upright, simple rim with a 'pinched' side strap handle with an undulating outer surface (Reduced Fabric 1, HC08 (*100*))

35 Smoothed bunghole from a cistern with textured outer surface (Reduced Fabric 1, HC09 (*1004*))

36 Slightly sagging, obtuse-angled base (with firing fault on the underside) (Reduced Fabric 1, HC08 (*112*))

37 Flat, obtuse-angled base (with firing faults on the underside) (Reduced Fabric 1, HC08 (*103*))

38 Obtuse-angled base, with firing fault from stacking; noted to be particularly crudely made (Miller pers comm.) (Reduced Fabric 1, HC08 (*113*))

39 Upright, gently ribbed rim, which is slightly thickened internally (Reduced Fabric 2, HC2010 TR3 (*08*) refitting HC10 TR3 (*40*))

40 Upright, simple jug rim, which is slightly thickened internally and has possible firing faults from stacking, with thumbed side strap handle with an undulating outer surface (Reduced Fabric 2, HC10 TR3 (*08*) refitting HC2010 TR3 (*40*) and HC2010 TR3 EXT (*83*))

41 Upright, simple, rounded, rim, with thumbed side strap handle (Reduced Fabric 2, HC08 (*119*))

42 Thumbed terminus of a side strap handle (Reduced Fabric 2, HC10 TR3 EXT (*85*))

43 Body fragments with an applied pellet and applied strap and stabbed decoration (Reduced Fabric 2, HC2010 TR3 (*08*) refitting HC10 TR3 (*12*))

44 Slashed smoothed bunghole (Reduced Fabric 2, HC09 (*1002*))

45 Body fragment with 'wavy' combed decoration (Reduced Fabric 2, HC10 TR3 (*08*))

46 Body fragment with combed decoration (Reduced Fabric 2, HC09 (*1002*))

47 Flat, obtuse-angled base (Reduced Fabric 2, HC09 (*1011*))

48 Splayed, flat base of a jug (?) (Reduced Fabric 2, HC08 (*109*))

49 Slightly sagging, obtuse-angled base (Reduced Fabric 2, HC08 (*102*))

50 Sagging, obtuse-angled base (Reduced Fabric 2, HC10 TR3 (*04*) refitting HC2010 TR3 (*16*))

51 Sagging, obtuse-angled base (Reduced Fabric 2, HC09 (*1001*))

52 Possibly slightly recessed or sagging, obtuse-angled base (Reduced Fabric 2, HC10 ET1 (*02*))

53 Obtuse-angled, slightly recessed base (Reduced Fabric 2, HC08 (*163*))

54 Flat, almost right-angled, thumbed base (Reduced Fabric 2, HC10 TR3 EXT (*85*))

55 Obtuse-angled, slightly recessed base (Reduced Fabric 2, HC10 TR3 (*40*))

56 Upright, ribbed rim of a jug, slightly thickened internally, with a pinched lip, and side strap handle with an undulating outer surface (Reduced Fabric 3, HC10 TR3 (*13*) (note: the sherd is clearly labelled HC2010 (*040*)) refitting HC10 TR3 (*16*))

57 Body fragment with square-rilled decoration (probably from the same vessel as 58 and 59) (Reduced Fabric 3, HC08 (*102*))

58 Body fragment with square-rilled decoration (probably from the same vessel as 57 and 59) (Reduced Fabric 3, HC08 (*102*))

59 Body fragment with square-rilled decoration (probably from the same vessel as 57 and 58) (Reduced Fabric 3, HC08 (*102*))

60 Dish rim; brown internally (from red slip) and unglazed buff-colour externally (Slip-coated ware Fabric 1: glazed red slip-coated buff-coloured earthenware, HC09 (*1004*) refitting HC09 (*1010*))

61 Burnt white slip-trailed rim (Slipware Fabric 1: brown-glazed red earthenware, HC09 [ET2?] (*1001*))

62 Refitting base fragments with white slip-trailed decoration (Slipware Fabric 1: brown-glazed red earthenware, HC08 (*125*))

63 Refitting bowl rims with white slip-trailed decoration (Slipware Fabric 2: glazed red slip-coated orange earthenware, HC10 TR3 (*02*))

64 Bartmann or 'Bellarmine' jug fragment, with beard and edge of seal and iron wash (1485-1714 if Frechen (Museum of London n.d.), but it could be a later English copy) (Non-factory-produced salt-glazed stoneware Fabric 1: salt-glazed grey-bodied stoneware, HC10 TR3 (*018*))

65 Rolled rim from small hollow-ware (Coarse earthenware Fabric 1: brown-glazed red earthenware, HC08 (*100*))

66 Rim (Coarse earthenware Fabric 1: brown-glazed red earthenware, HC08 (*125*))

67 Rim (Coarse earthenware Fabric 1: brown-glazed red earthenware, HC08 (*125*))

68 Possible bowl rim (Coarse earthenware Fabric 1: brown-glazed red earthenware, HC09 ET2 (*1001*))

69   Thin-walled hollow-ware (Coarse earthenware Fabric 1: brown-glazed red earthenware, HC08 (*101*))

70   Hollow-ware base (Coarse earthenware Fabric 1: brown-glazed red earthenware, HC08 (*100*))

71   Hollow-ware base (Coarse earthenware Fabric 1: brown-glazed red earthenware, HC08 (*125*))

72   Hollow-ware base (Coarse earthenware Fabric 1: brown-glazed red earthenware, HC10 TR3 (*04*))

73   Hollow-ware base (Coarse earthenware Fabric 1: brown-glazed red earthenware, HC08 (*125*))

74   Hollow-ware base (Coarse earthenware Fabric 1: brown-glazed red earthenware, HC09 (*1001*))

75   Hollow-ware base (Coarse earthenware Fabric 1: brown-glazed red earthenware, HC08 (*100*))

76   Hollow-ware base (Coarse earthenware Fabric 1: brown-glazed red earthenware, HC08 (*101*))

77   Crock rim (Coarse earthenware Fabric 2: black-glazed red earthenware, HC08 (*100*))

78   Crock rim (Coarse earthenware Fabric 2: black-glazed red earthenware, HC08 (*100*))

79   Crock rim (Coarse earthenware Fabric 2: black-glazed red earthenware, HC08 (*125*))

80   Crock rim (Coarse earthenware Fabric 2: black-glazed red earthenware, HC08 (*101*))

81   Crock rim (Coarse earthenware Fabric 2: black-glazed red earthenware, HC08 (*101*))

82   Crock rim (Coarse earthenware Fabric 2: black-glazed red earthenware, HC08 (*101*)

83   Crock base (Coarse earthenware Fabric 2: black-glazed red earthenware, HC08 (*100*))

84   Crock base (Coarse earthenware Fabric 2: black-glazed red earthenware, HC08 (*125*))

85   Crock base (Coarse earthenware Fabric 2: black-glazed red earthenware, HC08 (*100*))

86   Crock base (Coarse earthenware Fabric 2: black-glazed red earthenware, HC08 (*100*))

87   Crock base (Coarse earthenware Fabric 2: black-glazed red earthenware, HC09 (*1006*))

88   Pancheon rim (Coarse earthenware Fabric 2: black-glazed red earthenware, HC10 TR3 (*02*))

89   Pancheon rim (Coarse earthenware Fabric 2: black-glazed red earthenware, HC08 (*100*))

90   Pancheon rim (Coarse earthenware Fabric 2: black-glazed red earthenware, HC08 (*101*))

91   Pancheon rim (Coarse earthenware Fabric 2: black-glazed red earthenware, HC08 (*101*))

92   Pancheon rim (Coarse earthenware Fabric 2: black-glazed red earthenware, HC08 (*100*))

93   Pancheon rim (Coarse earthenware Fabric 2: black-glazed red earthenware, HC08 (*100*))

94   Pancheon rim (Coarse earthenware Fabric 2: black-glazed red earthenware, HC08 (*101*))

95   Pancheon rim (Coarse earthenware Fabric 2: black-glazed red earthenware, HC10 TR3 (*11*))

96   Pancheon base (Coarse earthenware Fabric 2: black-glazed red earthenware, HC08 (*105*))

97   Pancheon base (Coarse earthenware Fabric 2: black-glazed red earthenware, HC08 (*101*))

98   Pancheon base (Coarse earthenware Fabric 2: black-glazed red earthenware, HC08 (*100*))

99   Pancheon base (Coarse earthenware Fabric 2: black-glazed red earthenware, HC08 (*125*))

100 Pancheon base (Coarse earthenware Fabric 2: black-glazed red earthenware, HC08 (*100*))

101 Pancheon base (Coarse earthenware Fabric 2: black-glazed red earthenware, HC08 (*125*))

102 Mug or jug rim (Early brown-glazed red earthenware Fabric 1: low-fired brown-glazed red earthenware, HC10 TR3 (*016*))

103 Handle terminal (Early brown-glazed red earthenware Fabric 1: low-fired brown-glazed red earthenware, HC10 TR3 (*40*))

104 Refitting body fragments from a cup or jug with applied white slip decoration (Early brown-glazed red earthenware Fabric 1: low-fired brown-glazed red earthenware (slip-decorated), HC10 TR3 (*40*) (probably from the same vessel as *105*))

105 Cup or jug with applied white slip decoration (probably from the same vessel as *104*) (Early brown-glazed red earthenware Fabric 1: low-fired brown-glazed red earthenware (slip-decorated), HC10 TR3 (*40*))

106 Cup handle (Early brown-glazed red earthenware Fabric 2: olivey-brown metallic-speckled-glazed red earthenware, HC08 (*102*))

107 Body fragment with applied pellet (Early brown-glazed red earthenware Fabric 2: olivey-brown metallic-speckled-glazed red earthenware, HC2010 TR3 (*40*) refitting HC10 TR3 (*42*))

108 Cistercian ware Type 1? cup (Blackware Fabric 1: dark brown-glazed red earthenware with pitted surface and mid-brown/purple patches, with some metallic speckles, HC10 TR3 (*41*) refitting HC10 (*04*))

109 Cup with horizontal ridge; filed and re-used after rim breakage (Blackware Fabric 1: dark brown- glazed red earthenware with pitted surface and mid-brown/purple patches, with some metallic speckles, HC2010 TR3 (*34*) refitting HC10 TR3 (*41*))

110 Cistercian ware Type 1 decorated cup (?) fragment with horizontal ridge and applied white slip decoration (Blackware Fabric 1: dark brown-glazed red earthenware with pitted surface and mid-brown/purple patches, with some metallic speckles, HC08 (*103*) refitting HC08 (*106*))

111 Inverted concave hollow-ware rim (Blackware Fabric 1: dark brown-glazed red earthenware with pitted surface and mid-brown/purple patches, with some metallic speckles, HC09 (*1001*))

112 Cistercian ware Type 1? cup with upper handle terminal (Blackware Fabric 2: dark brown-glazed red earthenware with metallic speckles, overall dull metallic finish, or areas of dull purple, HC10 TR3 (*04*))

113 Cistercian ware Type 1? cup or jug base with lower handle terminal and applied white slip discs (similar decoration to Wrenthorpe decorative element 9 (Moorhouse and Roberts 1992, *92*)) either side of handle terminal (Blackware Fabric 2: dark brown-glazed red earthenware with metallic speckles, overall dull metallic finish, or areas of dull purple, HC10 TR3 EXT (*83*))

114 Fineware Cistercian ware Type 1? cup fragment with upper handle terminal (Blackware Fabric 2: dark brown-glazed red earthenware with metallic speckles, overall dull metallic finish, or areas of dull purple, HC10 TR3 (*09*))

115 Pedestal base of a fineware Cistercian ware Type 1? cup (Blackware Fabric 2: dark brown-glazed red earthenware with metallic speckles, overall dull metallic finish, or areas of dull purple, HC10 TR3 EXT (*84*))

116 Thin cup handle, close to the lower terminal, with thick white slip decoration (Blackware Fabric 2: dark brown-glazed red earthenware with metallic speckles, overall dull metallic finish, or areas of dull purple, (HC08 (*167*))

117 Crudely potted fineware cup (?) fragments with applied ridged white slip decoration (Blackware Fabric 2: dark brown-glazed red earthenware with metallic speckles, overall dull metallic finish, or areas of dull purple, HC10 TR3 (*016*))

118 Body fragment with applied rough and grog-rich white slip cross (Blackware Fabric 2: dark brown-glazed red earthenware with metallic speckles, overall dull metallic finish, or areas of dull purple, HC10 TR EXT (*83*))

119 Fineware hollowware cup fragment with applied rough and grog-rich white slip cross (Blackware Fabric 2: dark brown-glazed red earthenware with metallic speckles, overall dull metallic finish, or areas of dull purple, HC08 (*166*))

120 Everted cup (?) rim, burnt (Blackware Fabric 3: dark brown-glazed red earthenware without metallic speckles or dull metallic or purple areas, HC10 TR3 (*10*))

121 Cup (?) rim (Blackware (Fabric 4), HC09 (*1001*))

The Clay Tobacco Pipes,
by Peter Davey

The clay pipe was recorded and studied according to nationally agreed guidelines (Davey, 1981; Davey and Higgins, 1984). The two individual stamps were recorded and impressions submitted to the National Stamp Catalogue held at the University of Liverpool and all of the bowls, stamps and decorated fragments are illustrated in Fig. 43. A total of 84 fragments of clay tobacco pipe were recovered from 28 contexts. The assemblage includes 13 bowls or bowl fragments, 63 stems, five mouthpieces and three stem/bowl junctions. Some of the fragments were stamped with makers' marks or were decorated and in these cases it was often possible to specify a close date range. However, the context groups are small, with an average of three fragments per context, and in view of this it is not possible to make any chronological judgments with any degree of confidence, whether in terms of stem bore analysis or typological dating of forms and decorative variables (Davey, 1975). What can be said overall is that the collection ranges in date from the mid-17th to the end of the 19th century, with a scarcity of 18th century products. There are three bowls, two bowl fragments and at least 27 stems that appear to belong to the 17th century.

Bore Diameter Histogram Analysis
The pattern of deposition can best be seen from the histogram of bore diameters, especially when they are compared with other sites (Fig. 44). For example, compared with three different excavations at Norton in Cheshire, the Holme Cultram group can be seen as distinct. Norton Priory was a high status site founded on the Augustinian abbey. The histogram shows a wide spread of bore diameters with peaks at 7/64" and 5/64". This, and the forms of the pipes themselves, reflects a continued pipe use through the 17th century and a more intense

deposition in the early part of the 18th century associated with the building of the new house around 1730 (Davey, 1985; 2008). Lodge Farm in Norton Village was a toft that was occupied by buildings in the 17th century and subsequently incorporated into an agricultural plot that received pipes as rubbish fairly consistently until the end of the 19th century (Davey, 1977). The 1991 excavations of a plot in the village on the opposite side of the road received virtually no rubbish in the 17th century but produced a significant 19th century group.

Ordsall Hall in Salford has a stem-bore peak at 6/64", followed by 5/64", 7/64" and 4/64". This, together with the ceramic evidence, reflects a small quantity of residual, mid-17th century activity and the main excavated sequence belonging to the early and mid-18th century (Davey, 1980). Gristlehurst is a farm in Greater Manchester which was occupied continuously from the 16th to the 20th century. Clay pipe smoking there peaked in the middle of the 17th century and declined steadily thereafter.

Three castles – Pontefract, Barnard, and Beeston – demonstrate clearly how the stem bore histograms reflect differing phases of use from each other. At Pontefract the main deposits excavated belonged to the Civil War occupation in the mid-17th century, the remaining finds being attributed to tourists from the beginning of the 19th century. Hence the high peak of 7/64" and the small number of 4 and 5/64" bores (Davey and White, 2002). In contrast, at Beeston there was also a significant Civil War occupation and demolition deposit after which the castle was not occupied, except for a local family who moved into the outer gatehouse in the first few years of the 18th century. The very high peak of 4/64" bore is due to the presence of a shooting range using Chester-made clay pipes (William Boynton, manufacturer) which formed part of the annual fair on the site towards the end of the 19th century (Davey, 1993, 180).

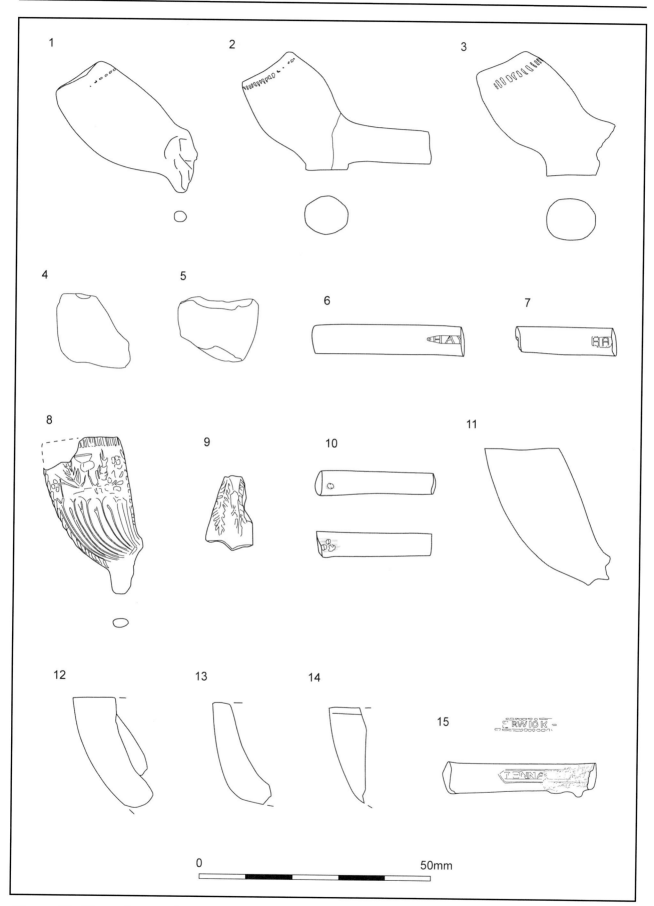

Figure 43: Clay tobacco pipes

Barnard Castle has the smoothest profile of all. Thus, although there is a peak in bore values that implies significant 17th century activity, the numbers of narrower bores indicate the presence of smokers on the site from then until the end of the 19th century. Given the known history of its occupation it seems likely that a good proportion of the later pipes were the possessions of visitors rather than residents as the site became a popular tourist destination.

The most similar profile to Holme Cultram is the one from Beeston Castle. The main difference is that the 17th century material from Beeston represents a period of intense occupation during the English Civil War. The earlier finds at Holme Cultram appear much more likely to be residual in character. The higher 5/64" values probably reflect activity in the later 18th century.

Discussion

This small group from Holme Cultram provides useful additional information about the supply and use of pipes in north-west Cumbria in the 17th and 19th centuries. In the 17th century the presence of Yorkshire-type products confirm their significance, especially in the north of the county (White, 2004, 554). At the same time the finding of late 18th century stamped stems from Liverpool emphasises the well established importance of the production centres in south Lancashire and the Irish Sea as a conduit of goods, services and technologies to Cumbria (cf. Weatherill and Edwards, 1972). The Tennant stem from Berwick and the Scottish style of the one complete decorated bowl reflect, perhaps, more northern and localised tobacco pipe supplies in the 19th century.

Catalogue of illustrated pipes

The illustrated pieces are listed below in approximately chronological order. The context number is written in brackets after each description:

1.	Spurred bowl, plain except for partial milling on the front; damaged bore. Although spurred forms are much more common in north-west, as opposed to north-east England, it is not possible to identify the origin of this pipe more closely than to say that it was almost certainly made in northern England 1650-70 (cf. Chester: Rutter and Davey, 1980, 68, Fig. 10, Nos. 103-107; Rainford: Davey, 1978, 6-7, Fig. 3, A to F, 1982, 2-3, Fig. 1, Nos. 4-6; Dagnall, 1990, 8, 21, 23; Wrenthorpe: Davey, 1992, 155-158, Fig. 81, Nos. 63-64, 73). On balance, given the width of the bowl and its relatively low quality it seems most likely that this is a south Lancashire product (HC10 ET1 (*02*))

2.	Bulbous bowl and part of stem in two joining pieces; large, flat heel, neat milling, otherwise plain; 6/64". This form is typical of Yorkshire products, though made in a larger area of north-eastern England, and dates from c1650-80 (White, 2004, 46-48, Fig. 6.5, No. 2) (HC09 (*1048*))

3.	Large bulbous bowl with crudely applied milling and a very large flat heel; 7/64". This too, is likely to derive from east of the Pennines but seems to be too poorly made to be from one of the major centres such as York, Hull or Beverley and dates from 1650-80 (cf. White, 2004, 48, Fig. 6.6, Nos. 4-8) (HC09 (*1063*))

4.	Bowl fragment; almost certainly dates from 1650-80 (HC10 ET1 (*02*))

5.	Bowl fragment; almost certainly dates from 1650-80 (HC08 (*101*))

6.	Stem fragment with part of a stamp applied parallel to the line of the stem; 4/64". The frame of the stamp is parallel sided but tapering at the end. The legend begins with a dot, in the tapering

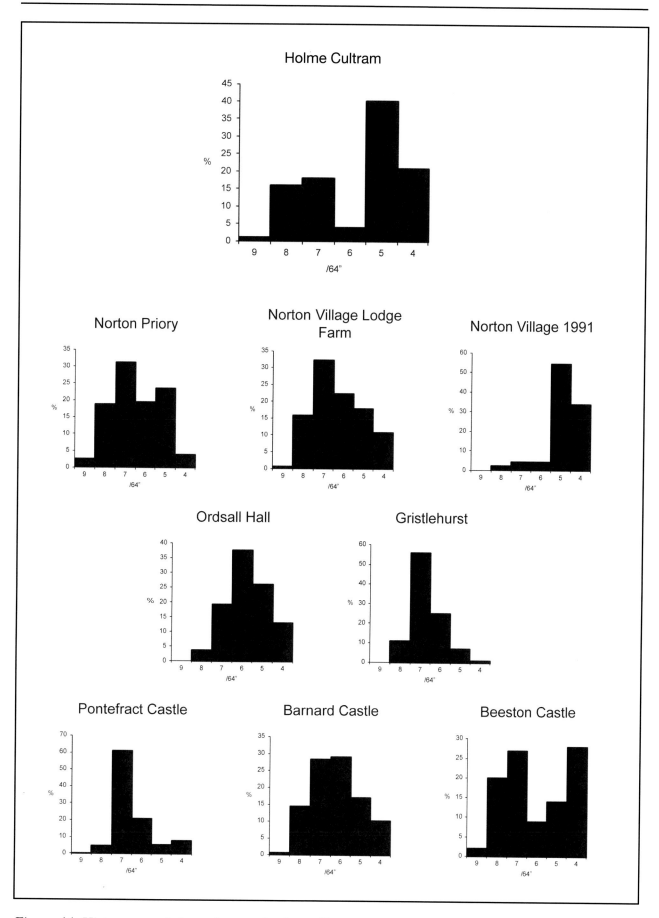

Figure 44: Histograms of clay tobacco pipe bore diameters

section, and then reads HA followed by a letter which might be the first part of a V or W but which, on close examination, is clearly a Y. This form of stamp and style of lettering is well known from Liverpool and Lancaster in the later 18th century. This example is very close to examples bearing the full name HAYES and the place LIVERPOOL (Coney 1980, 34-35, Fig. 2, No. 11). It is not known which of the Hayes family, who were active in Liverpool from at least 1774 to 1790, specifically used this stamp (Coney 1980, 37) (HC09 ET2 (1003))

7   Short piece of stem containing part of a very faint stamp at one end; 5/64". This appears to read as a dot followed by the letters HA. It may well be a further example of a Hayes stamp from Liverpool (cf. the preceding stem fragment) (HC09 (1001))

8   Mould decorated fluted and spurred bowl; 4/64". The fluting occupies the lower two thirds of the bowl and is well executed; the upper part of the bowl bears a thistle on either side; there is finely moulded milling around the top of the rim. This general style of decoration was popular in the first decades of the 19th century, especially in eastern England and Scotland (HC08 (100))

9   A small fragment of a mould decorated bowl with two raised ribs with pronounced leaf decoration (HC08 (100))

10   A stem fragment from just below the bowl/stem junction that retains a group of moulded dots both above and below; 4/64". The dots represent the end of the moulded design at the base of the bowl (HC08 (101))

11   This plain bowl, which has been heavily smoked, has a broken spur; 4/64". It dates from 1820 to 1840 and may have been made anywhere in Britain (cf. Atkinson and Oswald, 1969, 10-12, London Type 28) (HC08 (125))

12   Plain bowl fragment of 19th century date, but otherwise non-descript (HC08 (102))

13   Plain bowl fragment of 19th century date, but otherwise non-descript (HC08 (100))

14   Plain bowl fragment of 19th century date, but otherwise non-descript (HC10 TR3 (10))

15   Stem fragment, heavily encrusted with fire ash deposits; 4/64". Along either side of the stem there is a legend which reads TENNA.../...ERWICK. This is a product of the Tennant family of Berwick-on-Tweed who were working there from 1845-1918 and is likely to date from around 1900 (Hammond, 2009) (HC08 (100))

Report on the Coins and Tokens found at Holme Cultram Abbey Excavations 2008-2010

John Mattinson

One of the surprising things about the series of archaeological excavations at the site of the Abbey at Holme Cultram was how few coins were found and, of those that were, several were in such poor condition due to corrosion that they were not identifiable. As well as the coins lead tokens were found and these are also enigmatic. The coins are so few and the date range so large that they do not contribute much to our understanding of the Abbey.

Silver cut halfpenny – unidentifiable
HC08 *102*

Found in topsoil.

Silver pennies were often cut into halves and quarters (fourthings) for small change. This example of a cut halfpenny is so corroded that it is not possible to read any of the legend so cannot be identified.

Edward III first coinage penny (1327-1335) - tentative
HC08 *U/S*

This penny was found in the spoil heap and is very badly clipped so very little of the legend is discernable but it has been tentatively assigned to the reign of Edward III, first coinage from the Berwick mint. Three pellets appear in three of the quarters on the reverse but the fourth quarter seems to have a 'blob' rather than three pellets. This is possibly the bear's head that appears in one quarter on coins from the Berwick mint. Spink ref. S1535.

Silver penny Henry IV (1399-1413) or Henry V (1413-1422}
HC10 *40*

This was found in a robber trench for possible wall.

This penny is very corroded and none of the legend is visible. No details on the obverse of the coin are visible apart from a cross with three pellets in each angle and a 'diamond' in the centre of the cross. Because of the reverse design it has tentatively been assigned to the reign of either Henry IV or Henry V.

Edward IV gold Angel
HC10 *ext 85*

This was found in the medieval deposits at the bottom of the drain running east west on the 2010 site.

It is a gold angel of the second reign of Edward IV (1471-1483). It has an Annulet mint mark which dates it to 1471-1473. Spink ref. S2091

George III halfpenny 1806/07
HC08 *100*
Found in topsoil.
This coin is very corroded but the bust of

George III can be discerned on the obverse and Britannia on the reverse. Spink reference S3781.

Victoria penny 1874
HC09 *1005*

This was found in the south end of the trench, in the top of a disturbed area dating to the 19th century at the earliest.

This penny is much worn and it is not possible to discern many details except the date which is clearly 1874. Spink ref. S 3954

Leaden token
HC09 *1063*

This was found in the fill of the robbed out east -west inner cloister wall

This lead (or pewter) token appears to show a ship on one side (although this is open to interpretation) and the letters SEL on the other with a slightly raised rim on both sides. It was reported for identification to the Leaden Tokens Telegraph website and in the April 2010 edition of its newsletter. The newsletter can be viewed at http://www.mernick.org.uk/leadtokens/newsletters/LTT1004.pdf

60mm

Plate 22: lead token, obverse

93

It was initially thought "SEL" might have something to do with salt, as the monks were known to be involved in the salt trade on the Solway; however, I favour it standing for Selkirk, as the Latin for salt would be SAL rather than SEL. The object on the other side could be a ship, or a mitre; another reader has also suggested a bird or a monks 'cowl, although I do not feel convinced by either of these. Personally I slightly favour the mitre, as a symbol of ecclesiastic authority, although the ship is a very strong second candidate. Forgeais in Vol. 5 of his description of the Seine River finds (1866) identifies certain pewter pieces, depicting a semi ship like vessel, as having a fiscal purpose; these bear a limited similarity to this piece which also hints at a prow on the right hand side. Nick Holmes of the National Museum of Edinburgh comments "the use of the Gothic letter E would suggest a medieval rather than a post medieval date", with which opinion I would agree. I will guess at a date in the 15th or early 16th century, a little before the Dissolution of the monasteries; possibly not very much before. My preference is for the later part of that range; lettering (particularly multiple lettering) was not much in fashion on tokens in the 15th century and the S and L do not feel particularly early.

60mm

Plate 23: lead token, reverse

Leaden token
HC09 U/S

This token is badly corroded but does appear to have the letters SP?? on the obverse.

Metallic scrap
HC10ET1 *103*

Found in topsoil.

This metallic scrap is possibly the remains of a bronze or copper coin.

ENVIROMENTAL REPORT
Don O'Meara

The environmental evidence from the three years of excavations at Holme Cultram has been beset by the same problems encountered by other investigations into rural archaeological sites. Shallow stratigraphy over a free-draining soil does not allow the same preservation seen on urban sites of the same period. However, coupled with these taphonomic issues the site is also encumbered by the nature of its historical baggage. Due to knowledge regarding the history of the monastery's foundation, growth, dissolution and demolition there is the temptation to interpret the excavated material within the framework established by the historical record. However, the nature of the evidence means that much of the material being examined here derives from within demolition contexts, particularly during the 17th century. This disturbance means there has been much mixing of medieval, later medieval and post-medieval deposits; as evident in the report on the ceramic finds discussed within this volume. It is proposed here that the environmental evidence has raised a number of important issues for future research at this site. This may necessitate approaching the site with as much focus on the horizontal arrangement of artefacts and ecofacts, as on the vertical stratigraphic sequence.

The archaeobotanical analysis from the site has not produced remains which allow detailed inferences to be made regarding economically exploited plants such as cereals or wild plants which may have grown on the site. The one notable find, however, was the remains of deadly-nightshade (Atropa belladonna) from context HC10 *86* which is from a sample taken from the medieval deposits at the base of the drain running east – west. As a noted medicinal plant in the medieval period this may suggest the presence of a monastic garden near this area of the site. Cereal remains were limited to very low numbers of charred wheat and barley which do not add to our current knowledge regarding their importance in the medieval monastic economy.

From an archaeozoological perspective the animal bone remains allow suggestions to be made regarding spatial patterning of material across the site. Over three field seasons bone was hand collected and represents material which may be from either medieval table refuse, or from post-medieval and modern dumping. The remains of birds include domestic fowl, and domestic goose bones, as well as low numbers of Corvid species (crow family), partridge, pheasant, pigeon, passerine birds (general species of 'songbird') and woodcock and curlew. Wild animals included low numbers of red and roe deer, fox, rabbit and hare. Shellfish recovered mainly consisted of oyster shells with lower numbers of mussel and clam shells also recovered. Domestic animals included mainly cattle and sheep with lesser numbers of pigs and occasional dog, cat and horse remains.

There is no doubt that contamination of layers has occurred based on the pottery evidence. However, what is not clear is the extent to which this has affected the archaeozoological record. Discussion here will focus on the three main domesticates (cattle-sheep-pigs) with the suggestion that this demonstrates that some spatial patterning has been preserved across the site.

From the three main domesticates (cattle-sheep-pigs) approximately 550 bones were identified to their anatomical level. This equates to roughly 46% cattle, 46% sheep and just over 7% pig. This varies between the different phases of excavation. These figures correspond almost exactly to the ratios recovered from 2008, but in 2009 just over 50% of the bone was from sheep, with cattle bones representing just over 38% and pig bones representing over 11% of the three domesticates. From 2010, in contrast, over 50% of the bone was from cattle with about 44% from sheep and just over 5% from pigs.

Interpreting these remains is not straight-forward and numerous modes of interpretation are possible depending on which method of quantification is used. The interpretation here is based on impressions of the site during excavation and of the assemblage as it was being examined. Re-interpretation of these conclusions is possible by referring to the technical report and excavation archive.

Interpreting the remains of vertebra and ribs were an issue for all animals due to their fragmented nature. In particular rib heads were conspicuously low for all contexts and periods. For example, only one cattle rib head was recovered from the whole assemblage. Likewise, vertebra fragments were not particularly common considering the numbers which can be produced by a single individual; again taking cattle as an example only 26 vertebra centrums were recovered, as well as some fragments of neural spine and transverse process. Also, considering the low numbers of mandible, maxilla and cranium fragments recovered from the three main domesticates this suggests primary butchery was not being undertaken in this part of the site; rather the waste here represents prepared joints of meat. As an aside; over half of the dog remains were mandible or vertebral bones, showing that these remains reached their depositional contexts via a different route than that of the cattle, sheep or pigs (i.e not via consumption).

The raw data compiled from the recorded bones from the cattle-sheep-pig element of the assemblage is simplified in Table 6.1. This has divided the skeleton into 26 divisions in order to demonstrate the bias in favour of certain elements and the differences between the species. It can be seen that cattle bones are heavily over-represented by phalanges, with 70 phalanges recovered compared to 2 for sheep. With potentially 24 phalanges from a single animal this bias is significant in the interpretation of beef consumption at this site. An attempt has been made to compensate for this as can be seen in Table 6.2. Here 6 different skeletal zones have been chosen and their totals calculated. Division X is the number of times all the bones from the elements chosen occur in the skeleton of either cattle or sheep, while Result Y is the result of the Totals in the first column being divided by Division X (thus compensating for the bias). Sheep bones show a dense clustering around the articulation of the humerus and radius/ulna, as well as the lower half of the tibia and calcaneous/ talus. These elements represent over 55% of the bones recovered and may reflect patterns of consumption/disposal of these elements within the area of the monastery excavated. Likewise, the results for cattle show clustering around the distal humerus/proximal radius-ulna, and around the distal tibia-calcaneous-talus. The phalange bias has been much reduced by applying this method.

In Table 6.3 the year-by-year differences in cattle and sheep bone recovery have been tabulated. In some cases (and considering of course the different volumes of bone recovered from each year), these difference may reflect potentially significant differences in depositional activities. For both animals the recovery of scapula bones was much reduced in 2009, while in the same year bones of the pelvis were recovered in their greatest numbers. For cattle the recovery of talus bones is notably high for 2010, while for sheep femurs and calcaneous bones were both low for 2009.

Though the assemblage here is small compared to medieval bone assemblages from even some small urban excavations, it has raised many issues concerning patterns of consumption and deposition across the site. On rural sites such as these it is through these spatial patterns that past human activities may be detected. Should further excavation be undertaken at this site this line of research may be further pursued as a means to understand whether, in spite of subsequent disturbance, the patterns of monastic deposition has been maintained via the spatial patterning of the artefacts and ecofacts across the site.

Table 6.1

Element	Cattle	Sheep	Pig
Patella	3	1	
Phalange: Proximal	36		2
Phalange: Intermediate	21		
Phalange: Distal	13	2	
Humerus: Proximal			
Humerus: Midshaft	1	11	4
Humerus: Distal	9	36	3
Radius: Proximal	7	23	1
Radius: Midshaft	9	24	
Radius: Distal	3	5	1
Ulna	11	8	3
Acetabulum	9	16	4
Femur: Proximal	7	3	1
Femur: Midshaft	11	3	4
Femur: Distal	6	6	
Tibia: Proximal	3	7	1
Tibia: Midshaft	5	18	
Tibia: Distal	10	25	1
Calcaneous	18	17	1
Talus	12	6	2
Mandible	3	8	7
Axis/Atlas	5	3	
Metacarpal: Proximal	8	1	
Metacarpal: Distal	5		
Metatarsal: Proximal	4	7	
Metatarsal: Distal	3	1	
Scapula: Glenoid	15	10	1
Totals	237	241	36	514

Table 6.2

Cattle	Total	Division X	Result Y
Phalanges	70	24	2.9
Distal Humerus-Proximal R	26	6	4.3
Acetabulum-Proximal Fem	16	4	4
Distal Femur-Proximal Tibi	10	4	2.5
Distal Tibia-Calcaneous-Ta	40	6	6.7
Metapodials	20	4	5
Sheep			
Phalanges	2	24	0.08
Distal Humerus-Proximal R	67	6	11.1
Acetabulum-Femur	19	4	4.7
Distal Femur-Proximal Tibi	13	4	3.2
Tibia Midshaft/Distal-Calca	66	8	8.2
Metapodial	19	4	4.7

Table 6.3
Cattle

Element	2008	2009	2010
Calcaneous	3	5	10
Talus	1	1	10
Phalanges	16	17	37
Femur	6	4	13
Humerus	2	2	6
Innominate	3	5	2
Metapodials	8	7	13
Radius/Ulna	9	6	14
Tibia	4	4	11
Scapula	5	1	2

Sheep

Element	2008	2009	2010
Calcaneous	7	2	8
Talus	3	-	3
Phalanges	1	-	1
Femur	6	1	5
Humerus	7	17	23
Innominate	3	8	5
Metapodials	3	11	1
Radius/Ulna	13	20	28
Tibia	12	14	23
Scapula	2	-	12

Table 6: Environmental data; Cattle, sheep and pig assemblage

Metalwork From Holme Cultram Abbey

Tim Padley, Curator of Archaeology,
Tullie house Museum and Art Gallery Trust

LEAD

Drip
HC09 *1007*

An irregular hook-shaped piece of metal. There is a bulb at one end. The other end has a short projection at an acute angle to the main body of the piece.
L.36mm W. (max) 6mm

Lid
HC10 Trench 3 *04* SF 4 (Fig. 45.1)

A disc of lead (or a lead alloy such as pewter) with a tapering rectangular=sectioned ridge on one surface. The ridge suggests that it was a hinged lid from a vessel such as a flagon. However, there is no perforation through it. There is some damage to the edge of the disc.
Dia. 91mm W. (of ridge) 15mm (max); 8mm (min) Th. (edge) 1mm Th. (at the edge by the maximum thickness of the ridge) 14mm

Disc
HC10 *09* SF12

A disc of lead. There is a small perforation near the edge. Running from the perforation on one face is a line marking the diameter. Opposite the hole, the line is elaborated with incised irregular 'V'-shapes. To one side is an incised compass drawn circle with a central dot. The other surface appears blank.
Dia. 68mm Th. 2mm Dia. (of the hole) 3mm
Dia. (of the incised ring) 17mm

Small disc
HC10 ET1*02* SF102
Just over half of a small disc of lead. It has

irregular, turned-up edges. The 'concave' side is smooth, while the 'convex' side is rough and irregular. Possibly used on the end of something to 'pack' it.
Dia. 37mm Th. (max) 2mm

COPPER ALLOY

Mechanism
HC09 *1000*

Two pieces of a composite object. They join and suggest that the original was a circular sheet of copper alloy with a central circular perforation. There are three rivets with domed heads on the 'outer' surface. One is much larger than the rest. The two smaller ones hold a penannular piece of copper alloy sheet. The rivets run through a rectangular expansion on one side. The gap spans the larger rivet, but what was held is missing. One end of the curved piece has a pointed end at right-angles to the body of the piece. The precision of the piece suggests that it is of post-medieval date.
Dia. (main piece) 45mm
Dia. (central perforation) 6mm
Dia. (penannular piece) 21mm

Vessel/Float
HC09 *1001*

A thin-walled originally circular object. The whole is now bent and crumpled. The rim has a 'step' around it 6mm from the top which suggests that it could have been joined to another, similar piece. If this is the case it could be a small spherical float. If not, then it is probably the remains of a small vessel.
L. 60mm W. 48mm

Spur
HC09 *1004* SF160 (Fig. 45.2)

Fragment of the cast side and terminal of a spur. The fragment has a heart-shaped end with two circular holes through it. One of the holes is more worn than the other. Below this is a collar. The outer surface of the lenticular-sectioned spur side is decorated with two longitudinal lines infilled with incised 'V' shapes.

A similar fragment from Lincolnshire (NLM-D3AAF7) on the Portable Antiquities Database, has been dated to the 16th to 17th century.
L. 39mm W. (across terminal) 14mm
Th. (max) 3mm

Book fitting
HC10 ET1 SF160 (Fig. 45.3)

A book fitting which has a circular body with a pierced rectangle at one side and teardrop-shaped projection at the other. The projection has a transverse perforation through it. The plate is decorated on one surface with four dot-and-circle motifs arranged round a central perforation in a quatrefoil.

Similar items on the Portable Antiquities Database suggest 14th to 15th century date.
L. 37mm W. (max) 20mm
Dia. (central perforation) 3mm

Rectangular fitting
(Fig. 45.4)

Two rectangular plates of copper alloy with a central circular perforation. They are rivetted together with a rivet near each corner. The material between the plates has not been examined but may well be mineralised leather. It is not possible to say what the fitting is part of. However, given that similar, but more decorated items are classified as book fittings on the Portable Antiquities Database, it is possible that this is one.
L. 31mm W. 18mm
Dia. (central perforation) 5mm

Discussion

This collection of material comes mainly from the topsoil of the site. None of it is particularly diagnostic of any particular type of site. The majority is of post-medieval date and may have no connection to the monastic site at all. However, the book fitting and the second fitting if it comes from a book would not be out of place in a monastic context. The possible lid, though of interest, is not closely datable.

Note on nails
Pat Bull

The excavations from 2008-2010 produced a total of 241 nails. Most were heavily corroded and concreted. The nails which appear complete ranged in length from 35mm to 65mm. They were all hand made with rectangular shafts which tapered, where measurable from 5mm to 2mm x 3mm to 2mm. The heads where present were rectangular, or, in the larger type, round except for 8 which had a right angled bend top the shank at the top, typically 10cm long.

The round headed nails are tentatively identified as coffin nails as those found in 2008 were in the region of the graves. See appendix.

2008
Total nails found 65
Possible coffin nails 16

2009
Total nails found 66
Possible coffin nails 6

2010
Total nails found 103
Possible coffin nails 15 + 2 with large hexagonal heads.

99

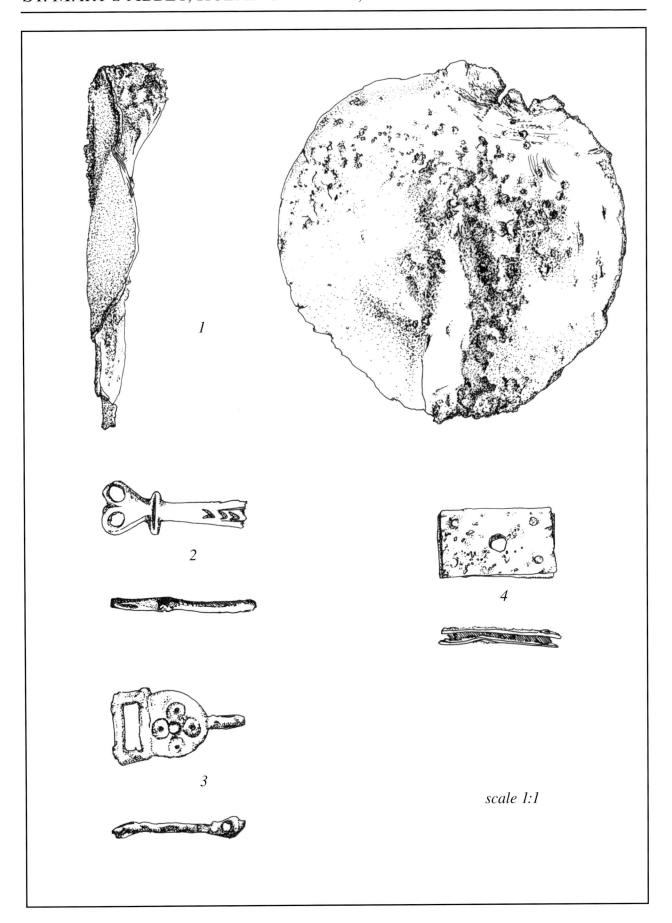

Figure 45: Metal objects

2010 evaluation trench 1
Total of nails found 7
A full analysis is available in the site archive.

Notes on post medieval bottle glass

The following contexts produced glass dating from the 18th century onwards.

HC08 *100*
4 fragments 19th/20th century glass
13 fragments early 18th green wine bottle including 1 with deep wide kick at base

HC08 *105*
15 body fragments dark green wine bottle

HC09 *1006*
1 fragment clear glass base
1 dark green body fragment

HC09 *1011*
1 fragment light green
1 fragment dark green wine bottle with deep wide kick, late 18th century

HC10 *02*
45 fragments of dark green wine bottle including 9 base fragments including 2 with deep wide kick dating to early 18th century
1 fragment of the neck of a wine bottle
3 fragments clear window glass
6 fragments of clear glass vessel
1 pale green base with pronounced kick

HC10 *03*
1 fragment window glass, clear

HC10 *10*
1 small clear glass ribbed jar
1 fragment pale green bottle neck
1 small green base with pontil
2 dark green bases with pronounced kick
2 dark green body fragments

HC10 ET 1 *10*
1 fragment dark green wine bottle body fragment.

Jet bead

A jet bead, conceivably from a rosary, was found in the medieval deposits of the drain running east–west. (HC10 *85*) It is oval in shape, 170mm long and 100mm wide, with a perforation through the length measuring 15mm.

Report on the Roof Tiles found at Holme Cultram Abbey Excavations 2008 -2010
Pat Bull

The roofing tile was mostly found in a 19th-20th century deposit in the 2009 excavtion. It seems likely that it originated from the cottages located until late 19th century on the western edge of the field south of the church, as shown on the 1865 first edition Ordnance Survey map.

Tentative evidence suggests some at least of the tiles were punched before firing with either a square hole or a round hole, or possibly both. This might mean the tiles were fixed more firmly and less likely to twist in a gale.

DISCUSSION

Mark Graham and Jan Walker

The fieldwork reported in this monograph shows the extent of disturbance to the monastic site and the 'efficiency' of stone robbing carried out after the Dissolution. Indeed, the trenches tell a story of the systematic removal of all valuable materials, though we should perhaps view this more as a process of re-cycling rather than destruction. Nevertheless, the extent of this activity meant that the vast majority of contexts encountered during excavations were of a disturbed nature and yielded a broad range of dateable pottery. Although a large amount of medieval material was recovered, this was often found associated with later pottery and so, while still adding to our knowledge of life at the monastery, cannot be placed in a secure context. Where intact medieval contexts were encountered, these usually consisted of substantial wall remains or flagged floors and were not excavated, but rather cleaned and recorded. During the first excavations in 2008 for example, none of the surviving floors, column base or walls were removed to search for earlier phases of construction. With so few fragments of the fabric of the monastery surviving, the removal of the last phase of building could not be justified on this scheduled monument.

The reference to Holme Cultram possibly belonging to the bishopric of Lindisfarne (Symeonis Dunelmensis, 1868, 66-8) carries the implication of early buildings on the site. Further, the monks were granted permission to source wood from Inglewood Forest in the foundation charter. No conclusive evidence of early timber buildings was found, though post holes found during the 2009 excavations are predating the monastic structure. There were also putative post pads in the area of the cloister, 2010 evaluation trench.

The earliest stone buildings had massive granite boulder foundations (2009 and 2010 excavations). The walling was of red sandstone blocks, possibly shipped from Scotland across the Solway Firth and up the River Waver. Later in the early 13th century the Abbey was probably rebuilt using local quarry stone, from near Aspatria, (Grainger and Collingwood, 1929, 23) which would mean that the repairs could be made locally after Scottish raids.

Heavy robbing of the desirable building stone both at the time of the Dissolution (1536–41) and throughout the 17th and 18th centuries means that it is difficult to identify phases of the rebuilding which must have taken place, especially after Scottish raids, as the stratigraphic record has often been destroyed.

Immediately Post-Dissolution considerable destruction took place; though records indicate some ruins still stood in the late 17th century (Denton, 1688). It is suggested that these may have included the arches of the eastern range, and that these fell in the late 17th–18th century, and can be traced in the architectural fragments layer *113,* HC 2008 excavation. Few square building blocks remain, so the stone has been sorted through and the moulded and less useful blocks left. The midden of oyster, whelk and assorted bones (*106, 107*) probably attests to the food discarded by demolition workers.

The lead cames of the window glass were probably melted down and sold. Dr. Tyson in her glass report suggests that the glass may have been removed at the time of the Dissolution demolition and dismantled in one area; if areas were cleared and the material then sorted this would account for the layer *09,* HC 2010 at the south end of the east range which was over a metre thick and this was where most of the glass fragments and also medieval tiles were concentrated. This dumped layer can be dated through pottery evidence to the 17th or 18th century.

Removal of stone from the site is well recorded with the last of the stone sold in 1688 (Denton 1688). Sporadic robbing of the site for stone continued as the local villagers looked for scarce building material throughout the 17th and 18th centuries, especially in the 2009 trench which is nearer the village (Grainger, 1910, 121, citing James Jackson churchwarden diaries).

Cistercian monasteries conform with occasional individuality to a similar plan. Part of the remit of the WCAS heritage lottery grant was the production of an interpretation panel for display at Holme Cultram. Figure 46 was initially designed for this purpose.

Remeasurement of their trenches and the WCAS excavations led to modification of the 1912 plan by Martindale. Comparative plans of Cistercian

Abbeys were consulted. Those of similar layout were Roche Abbey, Yorkshire, Dundrennan Abbey, Dumfries and Galloway, and of course Melrose, the mother abbey. The orientation of the refectory is conjectural and based on the fact that most Cistercian abbeys in the 12th and early 13th centuries orientated the refectory east west; orientation north–south seems to be a later feature.

The land at Holme Cultram Abbey constrains the building as it is surrounded by marshes and the river to the east and south. Investigation by magnetometry and by evaluation trenches revealed nothing in the way of buildings apart from the massive ditch to the north of the abbey (Fig. 8). A study of Millgrove Farmhouse to the south suggests medieval buildings extending to the east of Millgrove. It seems likely that apart from a possible further range of buildings close to the cloister to the south and extending from Millgrove, any development is to the west.

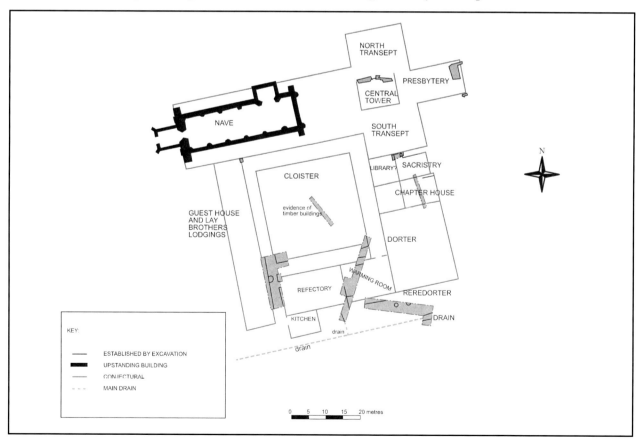

Figure 46: Interpretation plan; the Abbey layout in the twelfth century

Bibliography

Primary Sources
(CRO is Carlisle Record Office)

Bishop Halton's register CRO DRC/6/75/1

Boundary of Holm Cultram Abbey
1565 CRO DX 1`0/1

Denton, J 1687-88 History Manuscript– CRO
D/Lons/417/4/5/1

Enclosure Map 1814 for Holme Cultram Abbey
CRO SRDWB/1 (QRE/1/148)

Gough Map of Great Britain 1360 CRO R1.08

Greenwood Map 1821, 1822 CRO R1.08

Harrison and Fryer
1818 'Map of Cumberland' CRO R1.08

Holme Cultram Abbey pre Dissolution rental
and gressum book, 1519 CRO PR/122

Hodskinson, J., and Donald, T.,
1774 Map of Cumberland. CRO R1.08

National Monuments Record. – Historic
Environment Record, Kendal.

Ordnance Survey:
1864 1st edition Holme Cultram Parish
Cumberland Sheet XXVIII.2 1:2500
1900 2nd edition Holme Cultram Parish
Cumberland Sheet XXVIII.2 1:2500
1925 3rd edition Holme Cultram Parish
Cumberland Sheet XXVIII.2 1:2500

Martindale, J.H. and Sons,Architects, Carlisle,
*'Holme Cultram Abbey Restored plan of the
Abbey Church and Conventual Buildings'*
CRO DB6/Plans/1/49/1912

Jennings, N., unpublished notes on Millgrove
Farm deposited in CRO.

16th century Survey of the manor of Holm
Cultram (copy) CRO PR/122/200

Tithe map 1850 for Holme Cultram Abbey
Quarter CRO DRC/8/93/2

Secondary Sources
Alexander, J.S., 2004 'The Construction of the
Gothic Choir of Carlisle Cathedral, and the
Evidence of the Masons' Marks' *Carlisle and
Cumbria: Roman and Medieval Architecture,
Art and Archaeology. BAA Conference Trans.
XXVII*

Algar D. and Egan G., 'Balances and Weights'
Salisbury Museum Catalogue Part 3 (2001)

Allen, J., 2009a Panel of Geometric Grisaille,
c.1200-1250 *Vidimus,* 29 (May2009) Panel of
the Month, (ISSN 1752-0741 accessed
October 2010)

Allen, J., 2009b, An Excavated Angel from
Furness, *Vidimus,* 31 (July/August 2009),
Panel of the month, (ISSN 1752-0741, accessed
October 2010)

Anderson, A.O. ed. 1936 *'Chronicles of
Melrose'* London

Armstrong, A., et al 1950 *'The Place Names
of Cumberland'* English Place Name Society
Cambridge

Ashworth, A. 1887 *'The History of the Abbey
of Holm Cultram'* McMechan

Aston, M., 2000, *'Monasteries in the
Landscape'* Tempus, Stroud

Atkinson, D, and Oswald, A, 1969 'London
Clay Tobacco Pipes', *Journal of the British
Archaeological Association,* **32**, 1-67

Baxter, W., 1907 *'Archaeological* notes:
Excavations at Holm Cultram Abbey' *British
Archaeological Association,* Vol. XIII (N.S.13)
126-130

Blair, J., and Ramsay, N., ed. 1991 *'English
Medieval Industries'* Hambledon and London,
London

Blake, H, and Davey, P, 1983 *Guidelines for
the Processing and Publication of Medieval
Pottery from Excavations,* Directorate of
Ancient Monuments and Historic Buildings,
Occ Paper 5, London

Bloxam, M.E., 1843 *'The Principles of Gothic Ecclesiastical Architecture'* London

Bradley, J, and Miller, I, 2009 'The Medieval and Post-Medieval Pottery'. In C Howard-Davis (ed.) *The Carlisle Millennium Project. Excavations in Carlisle, 1998-2001. Volume 2: The Finds*, Oxford, 660-677

Brears, P, 1971 *The English Country Pottery: its History and Techniques*, Newton Abbot

Brisac, C., 1986. *'A Thousand Years of Stained Glass'* London, Macdonald

British History Online: Houses of Cistercian Monks The Abbey of Holm Cultram. http://www.british-history.ac.uk/report

Brooks, CM, 1999 'The Medieval and Post-Medieval Pottery'. In C Howard-Davis and M Leah (eds.) 'Excavations at St Nicholas Yard, Carlisle, 1996-7', *Trans Cumberland Westmorland Antiq Archaeol Soc,* 2nd series, **99**, 102-107

Brooks, CM, 2000 'The Medieval Pottery'. In MR McCarthy (ed.), 2000 *Roman and Medieval Carlisle: The Southern Lanes. Excavations 1981-2,* Department of Archaeological Sciences Unversity of Bradford, Res Rep **1**, Bradford, 139-143

Brooks, CM, 2010 'The Medieval Pottery'. In ML Hird and CM Brooks (eds.) *Roman and Medieval Carlisle: The Southern Lanes. Excavations 1981-2. Fascicule 3: The Roman and Medieval Pottery,* (http://archaeologydataservice.ac.uk/catalogue/adsdata/arch-979-1/dissemination/pdf/Complete_Fascicule_3.pdf), unpubl rep, 85-107

Brown, S., 1994 *'Stained Glass. An Illustrated History'* London, Bracken Books

Bulmer and Co. 1883 *'History and Directory of West Cumberland'* T.Bulmer and Company

Coney, A, 1980, 'M58: the interpretation of clay pipe scatters from field walking', *The Archaeology of the Clay Tobacco Pipe 3,*

British Archaeological Reports, British Series **78**, Oxford, 29-39

Coppack, G., 1998 *'The White Monks: The Cistercians in Britain 1128 -1540'* Tempus, Stroud

Cox, J.C., 1905 *'The Royal Forests of England'* London

Cropper, C., 2003 'Window glass' in A. Hardy, A.Dodd and G.D. Keevill, *'Aelfric's Abbey: Excavations at Eynsham Abbey, Oxfordshire, 1989-92'* Thames Valley Landscapes 16, Oxford University School of Archaeology, 330-40

Cunnington, P., 1990 *'How Old is That Church?'* Marston Magna

Dagnall, R, 1990 *An Illustrated Guide to the Rainford Clay Pipe Industry,* Rainford

Davey, PJ, 1975 'Stem Bore Analysis of Chester Clay Tobacco Pipes', *Cheshire Archaeological Bulletin,* **3**, 29-34

Davey, PJ, 1977 'Appendix Two: clay tobacco pipes', 83-93 in: JP Greene and PR Hough, 'Excavation in the Medieval Village of Norton 1974-1976', *Journal of the Chester Archaeological Society,* **60**, 61-93

Davey, PJ, *1978 Rainford Clay Pipes 1650-1750,* Institute of Extension Studies, University of Liverpool, Liverpool

Davey, PJ, 1980 'Clay pipes from Ordsall Hall, Salford'. In NJ Higham (ed.) *Excavations at Ordsall Hall demesne farm 1978-1979',* Greater Manchester Archaeology Group, Manchester, 26-33

Davey, PJ, 1981 'Guidelines for the Processing and Publication of Clay Pipes from Excavations', *Medieval and Later Pottery in Wales,* **4,** 65-88

Davey, PJ, 1982 'The Rainford Clay Pipe Industry: some archaeological evidence', *The Archaeology of the Clay Tobacco Pipe 7,* British Archaeological Reports, British Series **100,** Oxford, 91-306

Davey, PJ, 1985 'Clay Pipes from Norton Priory', *The Archaeology of the Clay Tobacco Pipe 9*, British Archaeological Reports, British Series **146**, Oxford, 157-236

Davey, PJ, 1992 'Clay Tobacco Pipes'. In S Moorhouse and I Roberts (eds.) *Wrenthorpe potteries: excavations of 16th and 17th-century potting tenements near Wakefield, 1983-86*, West Yorkshire Archaeology Service, Wakefield, 150-160

Davey, PJ, 1993 'The Clay Pipes'. In P Ellis (ed.) *Beeston Castle, Cheshire: excavations by Laurence Keen & Peter Hough,* English Heritage, London, 172-180; Fiche 2: G3

Davey, PJ, 2008 'The Clay Tobacco Pipes'. In F Brown and C Howard-Davis (eds.) *Norton Priory: monastery to museum excavations 1970-87,* Oxford Archaeological Unit, Lancaster, 371-375

Davey, PJ, and Higgins, DA, 1984, *Draft Guidelines for Using the Clay Tobacco Pipe Record Sheets,* unpubl rep (Copy in the National Pipe Archive, Liverpool University, Acc No. 1999.02.01)

Davey, PJ, and White, S, 2002 'The Clay Tobacco Pipes'. In I Roberts (ed.) *Pontefract Castle: archaeological excavations 1982-86,* West Yorkshire Archaeology Service, Leeds, 226-249

Duffy, S., 1995 'The first Ulster Plantation: John de Courcy and the Men of Cumbria' in Barry, T.B., Frame, R., and Sims, K (eds.) *'Colony and Frontier in Medieval Ireland'* Hambledon and London, London, 1-26.

Dugdale, W., 1817-30 *'Monasticon Anglicanum'.* Moran ed. Longmans

Eames, E.S., 1968 *'Medieval Tiles: a Handbook'* British Museum

Eames, E.S., 1980, *Catalogue of medieval lead-glazed tiles earthenware tiles in the*

Department of Medieval and Later Antiquities (British Museum) 2 volumes

Edwards, JEC, 2000 'Pottery Studies in the North-west 1975-2000 and Beyond', *J Medieval Pottery Res Group*, **24**, 40-8

Egan G., *'The Medieval Household, Medieval Finds from Excavations in London'* (1988) 311-317

Fawcett, R., 1994 *'Scottish Abbeys and Priories'* Batsford

Fawcett, R., and Oram, R., 2004 *'Melrose Abbey'* Tempus

Ferguson, C.J., 1874 'St. Mary's Abbey, Holme Cultram' *Trans Cumberland Westmorland Antiq Archaeol Soc.*, old ser, **1** 263 - 273

Forgeais, A., 1866 *"Numismatique Popuulaire"* Vol. 5 Seine River Finds Paris

Gilbanks, Revd. G.E., 1888 'The oldest register book of the Padrish of Holm Cultram,' *Trans Cumberland Westmorland Antiq Archaeol Soc* old ser. **10** 176-185

Gilbanks, Revd. G.E., 1899 *'Some Records of a Cistercian Abbey: Holm Cultram Cumberland.'* Walter Scott (London)

Goodman, A., 1989 'Religion and Warfare in the Anglo-Scottish Marches' Bartlett, R., MacKay, A eds *'Medieval Frontier Societies'*

Grainger, F., 1901 'The Chambers family of Raby Cote' *Trans Cumberland Westmorland Antiq Archaeol Soc.*, n ser, **1** 194- 234

Grainger, F., 1902 'The Holme Cultram Chapels' *Trans Cumberland Westmorland Antiq Archaeol Soc.*, n ser, **2** 335 – 347

Grainger, F.1903 'The sixteen men of Holm Cultram' *Trans Cumberland Westmorland Antiq Archaol Soc.*, n ser **3** 172-213

Grainger, F., 1921 'James Jackson's Diary 1650-1683' *Trans Cumberland Westmorland Antiq Archaeol Soc.*, n.ser, **21** 96-129

Grainger, F., and Collingwood, W.G, 1929 *'The Register and Records of Holme Cultram'* Cumberland Westmorland Antiq Archaeol Soc., Rec ser **7**

Greene, J.P., 1992 *'Medieval Monasteries'* Continuum

Greenlane Archaeology, 2011 *Holm Cultram Abbey, Abbeytown, Cumbria: Pottery and Clay Tobacco Pipe Analysis,* unpubl rep

Hall, D., 2006 *'Scottish Monastic Landscapes'* Tempus, Stroud

Hammond, P, 2009 'Tennant & Son, Tobacco Pipe makers, Berwick upon Tweed', *Society for Clay Pipe Research Newsletter,* **75**, 44-56

Harbottle, B 1964 *'Excavations at Newminster Abbey Northumberland 1961-3* Northumberland Press

Hare, R.N, 1985 *'Battle Abbey: The East Range and the Excavations' 1978-80'* Historic Buildings and Monuments Commission England. 80' English Heritage Archaeological Report no.**2**

Harrison, S., 2002 'Grey Abbey, County Down: a new architectural survey and assessment' *British Archaeological Association* 155, 115-167

Harrison, S., 2004 'The Architecture of Holm Cultram Abbey', Conference transactions *British Archaeological Association.* Vol 27 239-256

Hart, S., 2010 *'Medieval Church Window Tracery in England'* Woodbridge

Hodgkinson, D., Huckerby, E., Middleton, R., Wells, C.E., 2000 *'The Lowland Wetlands of Cumbria'* Lancaster Imprints **6**

Hodgson, T. H. Mrs 1907 ' Excavations at Holme Cultram' *Trans Cumberland Westmorland Antiq Archaeol Soc.,* n ser, **7** p.262 -268

Hutchinson, W., 1794, 'Parish of Holm Cultram' *'The History of the County of Cumberland and some places adjacent'* vol. 2. 327-348 Carlisle

Jamroziak, E., 2008 'Holm Cultram Abbey: a Story of Success?' *Northern History* **45** 27-56

Jamroziak, E., 2010 *'Spaces of Lay-Religious Interaction in Cistercian Houses in Northern Europe'* Parergon, University of Leeds.

Jarrett, MG, and Edwards, BJN, 1964 'The Medieval Pottery'. In R Hogg (ed.) 'Excavations at Tullie House, Carlisle, 1954-56', *Trans Cumberland Westmorland Antiq Archaeol Soc*, 2nd series, **64**, 41-57

Jennings, N., 2003 'Clay Dabbins: *'Vernacular buildings of the Solway Plain'* Cumberland Westmorland Antiq Archaeol Soc Extra Series Vol. XXX

Jope, EM, and Hodges, HWM, 1956 'The Medieval Pottery from Castle Street'. In R Hogg (ed.) 'Excavations in Carlisle, 1953', *Trans Cumberland Westmorland Antiq Archaeol Soc,* 2nd series, **55**, 79-107

Kerr, J., 1983 Window Glass, in A. Streeten, *'Bayham Abbey'* Sussex Archaeological Society Monograph **2**, 56-70

Kerr, J., 1985 The window glass in J.N. Hare, *'Battle Abbey: The Eastern Range and the excavations of 1978-80'* Historic Buildings and Monuments Commission for England Archaeological Report **2**, 127-38

Knowles, D., and Hadcock, N., 1953 *'Medieval Religious Houses in England and Wales'* Longmans

London Museum 1954 *'Medieval Catalogue'* HMSO

Lysons, D and Lysons, S., 1816 vol IV Cumberland, in *'Magna Britannia'* Cadell and Davies, London

Martindale, J.H., 1913 'The Abbey of St. Mary, Holme Cultram; recent investigations and notes on the ancient roof' *Trans Cumberland Westmorland Antiq Archaeol Soc.,* n ser, **13** 244-251

Martindale, J.H., 1925 'Holme Cultram Abbey, restored ground plan of the abbey church and conventual buildings, NMR.

Marks, R., 1993 *'Stained glass in England during the Middle Ages'* London, Routledge

Maxwell, H., (trans) 1913 *'Chronicles of Lanercost 1272 -1346',* Glasgow

McCarthy, M.R., and Brooks C.M., 1988 *'Medieval Pottery in Britain AD 900-1600'* Leicester UP

McCarthy, M.R, 1990 *A Roman, Anglian and Medieval Site at Blackfriars Street, Carlisle: Excavations 1977-9,* Cumberland Westmorland Antiq Archaeol Soc Res Ser Vol. 4, Kendal

McCarthy, M.R, and Brooks, CM, 1988 *Medieval Pottery in Britain,* AD 900-1600, Gloucester

McCarthy, M.R, and Brooks, CM, 1992 'The Establishment of a Medieval Pottery Sequence in Cumbria, England'. In D Gaimster and M Redknap (eds.) *Everyday and Exotic Pottery from Europe c.650-1900,* Exeter, 21-37

McCarthy, M.R, and Taylor, J, 1990 'Pottery of the Anglo-Saxon to Post-medieval Periods'. In MR McCarthy (ed.) *A Roman, Anglian and Medieval Site at Blackfriars Street, Carlisle: excavations 1977-9,* Cumberland Westmorland Antiq Archaeol Soc Res Ser Vol. 4, Kendal, 301-311

Medieval Pottery Research Group (MPRG), 1998 *A Guide to the classification of Medieval Ceramic Forms,* MPRG Occ Paper 1, London

Miller, A.T., 1972 *'A Short Guide to Holm Cultram Abbey, Cumberland.'* Cumberland.

Morris, R.K., 1978 'The Development of Later Gothic Mouldings in England, c. 1250 -1400' *Architectural History: Journal of the Society of Architectural Historians of Great Britain, Vol. 21*

MPRG, 2001 *Minimum Standards for the Processing, Recording, Analysis and Publication of Post-Roman Ceramics,* MPRG Occ Paper 2, London

Moorhouse, S, and Roberts, I, 1992 *Wrenthorpe Potteries: Excavations of 16th and 17th-Century Potting Tenements near Wakefield, 1983-86,* Yorkshire Archaeology **2,** Wakefield

Museum of London, n.d. *Ceramics Home: Stonewares: German: Frechen,* www. museumoflondon.org.uk/ceramics/index.asp

Neilson, G., 1974 *'Annals of the Solway Plain'* Whitehaven

Newman, RM, Hair, NJ, Howard-Davis, CLE, Brooks, CM, and White, A, 2000 'Excavations at Penrith Market, 1990', *Trans Cumberland Westmorland Antiq Archaeol Soc,* 2nd series, **100,** 105-130

Orton, C, Tyers, P, and Vince, A, 2008 *Pottery in Archaeology,* Cambridge, 10th printing

Paley, F.A., 1878 *'A Manual of Gothic Moulding'* London

Parker, F.H.M., 1909 'Inglewood Forest Part 4: the revenues of the forest' *Trans Cumberland Westmorland Antiq Archaeol* Soc old ser **9** 24-37

Parker, J.H., 1994 *'A Concise Glossary of Architectural Terms'* London

Platt, C., 1984 *'The Abbeys and Priories of Medieval England'* London Secker and Warburg

Platt, C., 1994 *'Medieval England; a social history and archaeology from the Conquest to 1600'* Psychology Press

Powell, D., *'Leaden Tokens Newsletter'* April 2010

Roberts, E., 1977 'Moulding Analysis and Architectural Research: The Late Middle Ages' *Architectural History: Journal of the Society of Architectural Historians of Great Britain, Vol. 20*

Robinson, D., ed. 1998 *'The Cistercian Abbeys of Britain: far from the concourse of men'* Batsford

Rutter, JA, and Davey, PJ, 1980 'Clay Pipes from Chester', *The Archaeology of the Clay Tobacco Pipe 3*, British Archaeological Reports, British Series **78**, Oxford, 41-272

Russell, J. C.1944 'The Clerical Population in Medieval England' *Traditio*

Ryder, P.F., 2005 *'The Medieval Cross Grave Covers in Cumbria'* Cumberland Westmorland Antiq Archaeol Soc Extra Ser **33**, Kendal

Ryder, P.F. 2010 *'Millgrove, Abbeytown, Cumbria; a Provisional Historic Building Survey'* unpublished (Kendal Record Office.)

Shoesmith, R and Richardson, R., 1997 *'Dore Abbey – a definitive history'* Logaston Press

Spink and Son Ltd., 2011, *'Standard Catalogue of British Coins, Coins of England and the United Kingdom.'* London

Stalley, R., 1999 *'Early Medieval Architecture'* Oxford UP

Stopford, J., 1990 *'Recording Medieval floor Tiles'* Council for British Archaeology Practical handbook 10

Stopford, J., 2005 *'Medieval floor tiles of Northern England Pattern and Purpose: production between the 13th and 16th centuries.'* English Heritage (Oxbow)

Summerson, H., 2011 'Edward I at Carlisle: King and Parliament in 1307' *Cumberland Westmorland Antiq Archaeol Soc* Tract Series Vol. XXIII Kendal

Summerson, HRT, 1993 ' *Carlisle: The City and the Border from late 11th to the mid-16th Century'* 2 vols Cumberland and Westmorland Antiq Archaeol Soc. Extra Ser, Vol. XXV, Kendal

Symeonis Dunelmensis, 1868 *'Opera et Collectanea'* Surtees Society Vol. 51

Tyson, R., 2000 *'Medieval glass vessels found in England c AD 1200-1500'* Council for British Archaeology Research Report 121

URL:http://www.British-history.ac.uk

Weatherill, L, and Edwards, R, 1972 'Pottery Making in London and Whitehaven in the Late Seventeenth Century', *Post-Medieval Archaeology*, **5**, 160-181

Whellan, W., 1860 *'The history and topography of the counties of Cumberland and Westmorland'*, London

White, A, 2000 'Pottery Making at Silverdale', *Trans Cumberland Westmorland Antiq Archaeol Soc,* 2nd series, **100**, 285-291

White, SD, 2004 *The Dynamics of Regionalisation and Trade: Yorkshire clay tobacco pipes c1600-1800: The Archaeology of the Clay Tobacco Pipe 18*, British Archaeological Reports, British Series **374**, Oxford

Whitehead, S, Williams, D, and Mace, T, *forthcoming* 'Excavation of Medieval Burgage Plots to the Rear of 130-136 Stricklandgate, Kendal', submitted to *Trans Cumberland Westmorland Antiq Archaeol Soc.*

Wilson, J., ed., 1905 *'The Victoria County History of the Counties of England; A History of Cumberland.'* Vol. 2 London

Winchester, A., 1987 *'Landscape and Society in Medieval Cumbria'* John Donald, Edinburgh

Appendix 1: Analysis report on the lead cames found at Holme Cultram Abbey excavations 2008 -2010

Joanne Wilkinson

Code HC--	Context	Inside width mm	Outside Width mm	Length mm	Junctions	Type	Milled/ Cast	Other comments
08	U/S							Round piece of lead- ring shaped
08	163	4	6	53		B	C	Piece that has bend in it
08	167					A	C	Very degraded- diamond flanges visible?
09	U/S			41		C	C	Very misshapen
09	U/S	3	7	30		C	C	Misshapen
09	U/S	3	6	28		C	C	
09	U/S	3	5	31	F	B	C	F shaped junction, bit misshapen
09	U/S	3	5	40		C	C	Misshapen piece, but not twisted.
09	1001							Very flat piece of lead, no profile visible
09	1002	3	7	123	T	B	C	Twisted
09	1002	3	5	75	Bent T	B	C	Twisted
09	1004							Too misshapen
09	1008							Very thin- half cames?
09	1011	4	7	57		C	C	Slightly Misshapen
09	1011	3	8	40		A	C	Diamond shaped flanges with hole 3mm long
09	1011	3	6	40		B	C	Misshapen
09	1019	4	6	26	Off centre T	C	C	
09	1019	5	8	45		A	C	Misshapen
09	1019	4	9	64		A	C	Very clear piece, can see diamond profile and join of cast
09	1019	4	6	45		C	C	Misshapen
09	Ext 2 010	4	8			A	C	Misshapen piece but appears to have diamond profile
09	Ext 2 016	3	7	56	(welded junction symbol)	C	C	2 pieces joined (welded?) together- repair? This refers to straight piece
09	Ext 2016	5	7	32	(welded junction symbol)	C	C	2 pieces joined (welded?) together – repair? This refers to the T shaped piece
09	Ext 1047							Not came, possibly strip used at the end of each sheet. Hole present
10	U/S Tr3							Very misshapen and twisted, plaster appears to be attached.
10	U/S	3	6	55		C	C	

10	09 Tr3	3	7	55		B	C	Misshapen and fattened-machined
10	09 Tr3	3	6	84		C	C	Slightly twisted with hole 3 mm long in one end
10	09 Tr3	4	7	113		A	C	Slightly twisted with a hole 6 mm long in one end
10	16 Tr3							Misshapen and squashed too flat- no profile visible
10	37 Tr3	3	6	29	T	B	C	
10	40 Tr3	4	8	66		A	C	Can see the diamond shape clearly. Broken through hole.
10	40 Tr3			105		B/C	C	What appear to be cast lines are visible
10	40 Tr3	5	7	87		C	C	
10	40/42 Tr3	3	7	43	⌐⊣ ⊢	B	C	The upside down F and sideway T are joined together. Slightly misshapen.
10	41 Tr3	3	6	27		C	C	Very misshapen to be sure
10	42 Tr3	4	6	65		C	C	Slightly misshapen half came that has twisted.
10	83 Tr3 Ext	3	7	35		B	C	
10	83 Tr3 Ext	3	6	54		C	C	Very twisted
10	83 Tr3 Ext	5	8	74		C or D		Very misshapen- bent to a V and twisted
10	84 Tr3	3	5	55		B	C	Slightly misshapen

Appendix 2: Roof Tiles found at Holme Cultram Abbey Excavations

All dimensions in millimetres
    Length - from nib edge
    Width - widest point
    Thickness - average of variation
    Edge if undamaged

H = hole
N = nib
LT and RT with underside facing
Nib to hole measured from centre of each
All measurements specific

Context		Whole	Nib	Hole	N - H	H - E	Upper	Lower
1020	Length	59	17				sandy	
	Width	105	45					
	Thickness	17	15					
	Edge	cut	cut					
	method		Hand					

Context		Whole	Nib	Hole	N - H	H - E	Upper	Lower
1019	Length	78	20	--			sandy	
	Width	109	67					
	Thickness	15	19					
	Edge	cut	cut					
	method		Hand					

Context		Whole	Nib	Hole	N - H	H - E	Upper	Lower
1019	Length	53	15	--			sandy	
	Width	84	45					
	Thickness	15	15					
	Edge		cut					
	method		Hand					
			Print					

Context		Whole	Nib	Hole	N - H	H - E	Upper	Lower
1008	Length	50	14				sandy	
	Width	95	45					
	Thickness	18	17					
	Edge	cut	cut					
	method		Hand					

Context		Whole	Nib	Hole	N - H	H - E	Upper	Lower
1002	Length	150	20	square	To Rt 30	68	sandy	
	Width	145	45					
	Thickness	15	15	Punch mark Pre firing L – U				
	Edge	Cut						
	method		Hand					
				12 x 12				
		Paw print						

Context		Whole	Nib	Hole	N - H	H - E	Upper	Lower
1008	Length	51	19					
	Width	55	38					
	Thickness	20	20					
	method		Hand					

Context		Whole	Nib	Hole	N - H	H - E	Upper	Lower
1026	Length	67	14	square	To Lt	-	rough	smooth
	Width	191	42	12 x 12	70			
	Thickness	18	15	Punch				
	Edge	cut	cut	L to U				
	method		Hand					
			Print					

Context		Whole	Nib	Hole	N - H	H - E	Upper	Lower
1011	Length	83	-				Rough	
	Width	111	48				?paw	
	Thickness	17	14				print	
	Edge							
	method		Hand					
			Worn					

Context		Whole	Nib	Hole	N - H	H - E	Upper	Lower
1026	Length	166	12	Trace	To Rt		worn	
	Width	167	135	round	c50			
	Thickness	12	17					
	Edge		cut					
	method		Hand					

Context		Whole	Nib	Hole	N - H	H - E	Upper	Lower
1011	Length	44	14				worn	worn
	Width	55	47					
	Thickness	14	c12					
	Edge	-						
	method		Hand					

Context		Whole	Nib	Hole	N - H	H - E	Upper	Lower
1019	Length	170	15				Sandy	smooth
	Width	172	145					
	Thickness	15	17					
	Edge	cut	cut					
	method							

Context		Whole	Nib	Hole	N - H	H - E	Upper	Lower
1011	Length	162	-				Worn+ +	worn
	Width	158	-					
	Thickness	c12	17					
	Edge		cut					
	method		Hand					
	diameter							
	Surface Worn++		part					

Context		Whole	Nib	Hole	N - H	H - E	Upper	Lower
1011	Length	150	17				Worn+	smooth
	Width	153	c140					
	Thickness	17	17					
	Edge		cut					
	method		Hand					
	surface	Worn+						

Context		Whole	Nib	Hole	N - H	H - E	Upper	Lower
1002	Length	60	15	Part Round dia 12	Lt 45		worn	worn
	Width	87	45					
	Thickness	12	c16					
	Edge	cut	cut					
	method		Hand					

Context		Whole	Nib	Hole	N - H	H - E	Upper	Lower
1011	Length	54	c11					
	Width	95	c142					
	Thickness	15	20					
	Edge	cut						
	method		Hand					
	surface		damage					

Context		Whole	Nib	Hole	N - H	H - E	Upper	Lower
1005	Length	55	17				sandy	smooth
	Width	53	-					
	Thickness	17	12					
	Edge	-						
	method		Hand					
			part					

Context		Whole	Nib	Hole	N - H	H - E	Upper	Lower
1011	Length	205		Square Rt 12 x 12			sandy 3 prints	smooth
	Width	256	Broken off					
	Thickness	14						
	Edge							
	method		Hand					

Context		Whole	Nib	Hole	N - H	H - E	Upper	Lower
1002	Length	60	trace	Rt			sandy	smooth
	Width	66		Round				
	Thickness	19		Trace				
	Edge			of				
	method			punch				

Context		Whole	Nib	Hole	N - H	H - E	Upper	Lower
1008	Length	90	--	Square		28	rough	smooth
	Width	200		12 x 12				
	Thickness	12						
	Edge			27from				
	method	Lt hand corner		top				

Context		Whole	Nib	Hole	N - H	H - E	Upper	Lower
1008	Length	65	-	Round			rough	smooth
	Width	80						
	Thickness	14 ?cut		dia 12				
	Edge							
	method							
	Damage by square punch to upper surface							

Context		Whole	Nib	Hole	N - H	H - E	Upper	Lower
1040	Length	85		Round		32	sandy	smooth
	Width	62		dia 9				
	Thickness	12		15				
	Edge			from				
	method			top				
	? Rt hand corner							

Context		Whole	Nib	Hole	N - H	H - E	Upper	Lower
1040	Length	81	18	Trace				
	Width	62	C42	to Lt				
	Thickness	12	12					
	Edge							
	method		hand					
	Finger prints on nib							

Context		Whole	Nib	Hole	N - H	H - E	Upper	Lower
1008	Length	92	-	Square 14 x 14		36 and 26		
	Width	73						
	Thickness	14						
	Edge	cut						
	method							
Corner ? Lt or Rt								

Context		Whole	Nib	Hole	N - H	H - E	Upper	Lower
1010	Length	64		Square 12 x 12		66 from side	sandy	smooth
	Width	89						
	Thickness	14						
	Edge							
	method							

Context		Whole	Nib	Hole	N - H	H - E	Upper	Lower
1011	Length	215		--			sandy	smooth
	Width	75						
	Thickness	12						
	Edge							
	method							
2 finger prints on under side to edge bent								

Context		Whole	Nib	Hole	N - H	H - E	Upper	Lower
1011	Length	95		Part Square 12			rough	smooth
	Width	21						
	Thickness	20						
	Edge							

Context		Whole	Nib	Hole	N - H	H - E	Upper	Lower
1011	Length	75					sandy	
	Width	60						
	Thickness	14						
	Edge							
	method							

Context		Whole	Nib	Hole	N - H	H - E	Upper	Lower
1019	Length	49					worn	smooth
	Width	58						
	Thickness	17						
	Edge							
	method							
Corner of square hole								

Context		Whole	Nib	Hole	N - H	H - E	Upper	Lower
1005	Length	75		Square 12 x 12			rough	
	Width	65						
	Thickness	12						
	Edge							
	method							

Context		Whole	Nib	Hole	N - H	H - E	Upper	Lower
1002	Length	34					rough	
	Width	34						
	Thickness	14						
	Edge							
	Corner of square hole							

Context		Whole	Nib	Hole	N - H	H - E	Upper	Lower
1019	Length	63		Round part			rough	
	Width	51						
	Thickness	14						
	Edge							

Context		Whole	Nib	Hole	N - H	H - E	Upper	Lower
1011	Length	53					worn	smooth
	Width	68						
	Thickness	16						
	Edge							
	Part square hole							

Context		Whole	Nib	Hole	N - H	H - E	Upper	Lower
1011	Length	59					sandy	smooth
	Width	54						
	Thickness	13						
	Marks in lower surface							

Context		Whole	Nib	Hole	N - H	H - E	Upper	Lower
1019	Length	99						
	Width	46						
	Thickness	12						
	Edge							
	Part square hole							

Context		Whole	Nib	Hole	N - H	H - E	Upper	Lower
1011	Length	62		12			sandy	worn
	Width	52						
	Thickness	14						
	Edge							
	Part square hole							

Context			Whole	Nib	Hole	N - H	H - E	Upper	Lower
1022	Length		74					worn	smooth
	Width		69						
	Thickness		14						
	Edge								
	? finger prints on under side								

Context			Whole	Nib	Hole	N - H	H - E	Upper	Lower
1011	Length		90					sandy	
	Width		73						
	Thickness		14						
	Edge								
	Finger prints								

Context			Whole	Nib	Hole	N - H	H - E	Upper	Lower
1010	Length		81	-				sandy	smooth
	Width		59	40					
	Thickness		14	-					
	Edge								
	Nib damaged - tile broken								

A

Abbeys:

Battle	57, 58, 60, 62, 63, 107	Grey	107
Bayham	58, 62, 107	Hailes	57
Bordesley	21, 57	Kirkstall	57
Bradwell	61	Lanercost	39, 108
Calder	57	Melrose	1, 3, 4, 5, 7, 103, 104, 106
Citeaux	4	Newminster	57
Dundrennan	24, 103	Rievaulx	3, 31, 41,
Eynsham	58, 105	Roche	2, 24, 103
Fountains	39	Warden	57
Furness	7, 59,	Westminster	4, 56, 57, 58
Garendon	58		

Abbey Cowper	1
Abbeytown	1, 8, 15, 38, 107, 109
Adamnan	4
Aelred of Rievaulx	3
Affreca	6
ambulatory	2, 4
Angerton	2
antiquarian	13, 51, 52, 53
Applegarth	iv, viii, viii, 1, 3,15, 17, 18
arcade	2, 9, 43
arch	8, 21, 31, 33, 34, 38, 39, 42, 61, 62, 102, 105
architectural fragments	21, 30, 38, 102
artefacts	1, 35, 94, 96
Aspatria	3, 5, 102
Aspinall, A	15
Augustinians	3, 88

B

bailiff	7
barley	95
Baxter, Revd W.	9, 10, 11, 30, 104, 107
bead	58, 63, 101
Benedictines	4
Berwick	90, 92, 93, 107
Beverley	90
bones, animal	21, 95
book fitting	99
Borrodaile, Gawain	7
Boston	6
bottle glass	101
boundary	2–3, 10, 17, 25, 30, 32, 35, 104
Bradford University	15
Broughton, D.	vii
Browning, L.	15, 16
Bull, P.	vii, 1, 99, 101
bungholes	70, 74, 83, 84, 85
burgh	6
Butler, L.	vii, 37

119

C